T0277812

UNBECOMING A LADY

UN-
BECOMING
A
LADY

THE FORGOTTEN SLUTS AND
SHREWS WHO SHAPED AMERICA

THERESE ONEILL

ILLUSTRATIONS BY LISA JONTÉ

SIMON ELEMENT

New York   London   Toronto   Sydney   New Delhi

SIMON
ELEMENT

An Imprint of Simon & Schuster, LLC
1230 Avenue of the Americas
New York, NY 10020

First Simon Element hardcover edition March 2024

SIMON ELEMENT is a trademark of Simon & Schuster, LLC

Simon & Schuster: Celebrating 100 Years of Publishing in 2024

For information about special discounts for bulk purchases, please contact Simon & Schuster Special Sales at 1-866-506-1949 or business@simonandschuster.com.

The Simon & Schuster Speakers Bureau can bring authors to your live event. For more information or to book an event, contact the Simon & Schuster Speakers Bureau at 1-866-248-3049 or visit our website at www.simonspeakers.com.

Interior design by Laura Levatino

Manufactured in the United States of America

10 9 8 7 6 5 4 3 2 1

Library of Congress Cataloging-in-Publication Data has been applied for.

ISBN 978-1-9821-9970-8
ISBN 978-1-9821-9971-5 (ebook)

In my life, I've known many women who got what they needed through unconventional means.

Of these,

TONI
LIZ
ALISON
SERRINA
LISA
SONJA
MAREN
CASSANDRA

. . . were just *the worst*.
Thank you so much for all you taught me.

CONTENTS

AUTHOR'S NOTE

Most of the women in these profiles lived around the turn of the twentieth century. Terms we may find offensive today were commonly used in the primary documents my researched is based on. I apply those terms only where they are historically integral.

INTRODUCTION

**UPON FINDING ONESELF TO BE PLAIN,
CRANKY, A BIT SELF-ABSORBED,
AND A TAD SLUTTY**

My friend, when I tell you that you're ugly, I say it with only compassion in my heart.

Now, don't get emotional. You're so temperamental. *Loud*, even. That's not desirable, either. I just thought you should hear it from someone who cares.

Hear what exactly? Well, you know.

You don't *fit*. Aside from your multitude of physical shortcomings and social blunderings, you've got weird hobbies, unsavory companions, and . . . well, forgive my bluntness, but the way you're tilting your head just now makes you look like an absolute whore. I'm sorry. If there were a gentler word, I'd use it.

You're not the woman you ought to be.

But you already knew that.

You've known that since you were a child, when a shampoo commercial made you understand that your hair was not even close to ebullient. You probably hadn't even known that your hair was required to exist as a joyous singularity, but I bet you've never forgotten. You've been compiling your near-constant failures as a woman ever since.

You know what a woman is supposed to be.

She:

TAKES UP JUST THE RIGHT AMOUNT OF SPACE. Small is best. You need to prove yourself worthy of the molecules you displace, madam.

IS PRETTY. You've a bit of luck, here! Twenty-first-century America has opened the definition of *pretty* wider than ever before! You can be pretty no matter your (flawlessly smooth) skin tone, and you can now have one of *two* different breast sizes and still be fashionable! (Cheekbone rise, eye shape and spacing, lip plumpness, and neck length remain nonnegotiable, however. Also, stop aging; it's a degrading habit.)

DOESN'T TALK TOO MUCH. And when she does so, we'd prefer she use the upspeak of a teenage girl asking for an extension on a school essay. Using a childlike tone makes your ideas more palatable for others to hear. So, if you must speak, do so thusly: "Because sometimes? Like, I think it would be a good idea? To put fire extinguishers on *all* floors of the building? But only if, like, . . . you guys are cool with that?"

DON'T SEEK UNSEEMLY PLEASURES, like alcohol, sex, or notoriety.

DON'T BE A FRUMPY KILLJOY, ruining anyone else's chance to enjoy alcohol, sex, or notoriety.

BE VERY SEXY BUT PRETEND YOU DON'T KNOW IT. Then stop, because you're being needy. Okay, now start again; it's fashionable this month to be sexually progressive. Wait . . . no, that one music video awards performance took it too far; you need to stop again. But any minute now an influencer will show a quarter inch of under-butt cellulite on TikTok and be called "brave," so you best keep some thongs handy.

Tired, yet? You should be because the rules are exhausting.

You're living in the most permissive and progressive era this planet has ever known. Imagine the rules for "good women" as they existed 150 years ago.

Now, imagine being the kind of woman who ignored those rules while pursuing marvelous things.

Imagine being plain, cranky, a little bit self-absorbed, and a tad slutty at the turn of the twentieth century.

Go ahead! It oughtn't be hard! "Plain, cranky, selfish sluts" describes most people to some degree! In fact, we could just shorthand "plain cranky selfish sluts" to "humans," if we wanted.

It's odd that history has had so little to say about women with an over-abundance of humanity. There is limited space for Women in History, and most of it has gone to silent beauties, righteous over-achievers, and literal saints.

Because, at the risk of invalidating thousands of bumper stickers, the truth is: well-behaved women *almost exclusively make history*. Women from Cleopatra to Ruth Bader Ginsburg found their place in history by doing what was expected and allowed—just doing it extremely well.

We've let history misplace so many fascinating stories. Achievements and adventures belonging to women who were not beautiful or mythically competent. Amazing, and utterly unsuitable American women.

I found a large deposit of these chipped and dusty diamonds dwelling in the mid-nineteenth to early twentieth centuries. This is a time when Americans had the most leisure, education, and money they'd ever known. As a result, women began to leave the homestead and look for things to do. Many of those things were considered "unladylike."

So, one "human" to another, let me introduce you to a few fabulous women whom history didn't much care for.

What follows are the stories of eighteen unique women. Women who had no virtue—or so much virtue that they decided to shove their excess down other people's throats. Women who were selfish—or so selfless it bordered on a psychological condition. Women who stuck their powdered noses into men's affairs and gummed up entire industries, changing them forever. Women who did magnificent things but who were really weird in their personal lives.

They were unbecoming as women; and they changed forever what women could become.

1.

MAKING A SPECTACLE OF ONESELF

**DARING DRAMA QUEENS
OF DUBIOUS RENOWN**

Without social media, if a lady of latter days wanted to be lauded for her charms, she would take to the stage. As with social media, audiences often found those attention-seeking ladies obnoxious. Cathartically so. A person can take a lot of comfort in feeling quietly superior to show-offs.

In this chapter we meet performers who were especially disreputable for their time and place. They desired attention more than anything else, and they were willing to sacrifice privacy, decorum, and perhaps a smidgeon of personal dignity to get it. They lived out of suitcases, kept disreputable company, were harassed and jeered at. They were also *paid*. These women put a whole new spin on the question of exploitation in the performative arts. Who is the real unfortunate soul—the strutting shameless peahen, *or* . . . the fella who hands that hen his paycheck just for the pleasure of watching her preen?

CELESTA GEYER

Whether skinny or near immobile from your girth,
you've got to honor your time on this earth.

A s a child, Celesta was her father's darling, and she went with him to his popular German pub nearly every day. She bounded between tables of friendly customers, being rewarded with food for her cuteness. The scientific term for Celesta's making such early psychological connections among food, making people laugh, and happiness is known as, "Oh, Girl, I See Where This Is Going." (Check the *DSM-5* on that, but I'm pretty sure you'll find it.)

At age six, in 1907, she started school. There, she learned the most important lesson of her life. She was fat, and that was bad.

For the next forty years people would remind her constantly and viciously of her size, and how it symbolized a greater failure. There's a special sort of anger humans have toward people who won't blend in, especially if they think it's by choice.

Dolly at eight years old

Fat or thin, Celesta was never, ever meant to blend in. She wasn't made for a passive life. She loved people, new experiences, and challenges. She also happened to love food.

Celesta quit school at sixteen, after having to sit at the front of the classroom in a special extended desk. Being up front proved too much of a distraction; since they could see her, the other students, and some teachers, tortured her all day. She went to work instead.

Celesta did the factory work that was common for girls of the era; she packed chocolates or soap. She even tried to work at the telephone company, but at 255 pounds she was told she wouldn't be able to sit on the switchboard stools all day. She left the safe circle of her family and began the adventure of youth; she became a successful Miami beautician and makeup model. Her face was large, but very pretty, and the cosmetics sellers thought her dimensions highlighted how their products could flatter.

She made friends, though she admitted many were a bit seedy. Her fatness made her seedy, too. She explored Tijuana with part-time prostitutes and "bad boys" who smuggled 1910s era *"la ma-ri-huan-a"* across the border.

Celesta enjoyed being alive, even if it was in a body the world didn't think deserved that privilege. Celesta won prizes at costume balls, she joyrided in cars (which is significantly more daring when you remember cars had been invented the previous decade), she rode horses despite not fitting the saddle. She turned down quite a few offers of sex work—something she'd keep doing most of her life.

By her early twenties she wanted to go back to her family and build a calmer existence. But the thing about "calm" is that it tends to be boring.

Well, one part of it wasn't boring. She found real love in a man named Frank Geyer, though she was suspicious of that love. She didn't know why he was marrying a 300-pound pariah. She made Frank procure a home, furniture, a good job, and a ring before she'd marry him, simultaneously proving she actually valued herself while giving him incentive to quit her. It didn't work. He loved her, and they were married happily until his death in 1967.

There wasn't much love for Celesta outside her warm family circle, however. Every time she left her house, Celesta had to be prepared for an assault of sniggers, stares, and screamed insults. It wasn't worth it. She stayed put and grew larger.

One day, as the Great Depression put the squeeze on her and Frank's finances, the couple went out to a near-empty local carnival. The barker in front of the Fat Lady tent called out to her. She cringed, but she had learned that when the world keeps screaming about how fat your butt is, sometimes you have to turn around and invite them to kiss it.

She wrote, "My courage dropped and my heart sank . . . but I took hold of myself and when we were within a few feet of him I boomed out, 'Do you want to see a real 338 pounds fat lady? I'll bet I'm a lot fatter than the one you have.'"

The barker laughed and waved the couple through the tent. Inside, Celesta met the 700-pound woman who would become her mentor, Jolly Pearl Stanley.

Jolly Pearl put voice to the truth that Celesta's life had centered on.

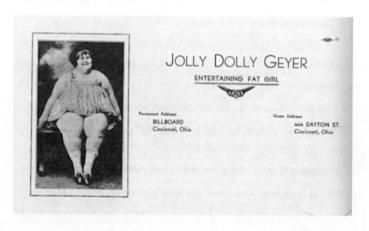

Dolly's advert in Billboard *magazine*

"You know, honey, everyone laughs at you now. Don't you think it would be a good idea to make them pay for their fun?"

It was a very good idea. Celesta became Dolly Dimples, "The World's Most Beautiful Fat Lady." She and Frank rode out the worst of the Depression in private Pullman cars, touring Hawaii, spending summers in a well-appointed tent in the center of the carnival's community. Celesta wore the satiny costumes she'd always loved, danced, sang, and sass-mouthed—and people laughed.

They were laughing at her, make no mistake. Just like they always had. She could not prevent that. The difference was that now they were giving up their Depression-era cash to do it. They were in *Dolly's house*, now.

This was illustrated by an incident she describes in her autobiography, *Diet or Die*, when a particularly rude lady asked: "How can your husband possibly make love to you?"

Dolly tossed off: "Why, honey, he waits until I go to the bathroom and then he follows the stream to the exact spot."

Celesta insists, "I wasn't proud of this answer [oh, she *totally* was], so in reply to the same question in Mobile, Alabama, . . . I was a bit more discreet. 'Mother gave my husband a blueprint of my body as a wedding present.'"

In the off-season, Celesta didn't rest on her ever-growing laurels. (She was 4 feet 11 inches and around 500 pounds when in her forties.) She and Frank bought a gas station in Florida, she put out her shingle as a psychic, and she became "Madame Celeste."

Painting on the side of the Dolly Dimples Show tent,
designed by Celesta herself

Celesta didn't believe she was psychic. But she had honed a useful skill that is often found in people who live lives wary of harm from others. Empathy. The ability to read humans.

Psychic translated into backwoods 1940s language as *psychiatrist*. She listened carefully, watched body language, used common sense, and helped. People flooded to her with problems ranging from picking lotto numbers to healing deaf children. Her largest clientele was African Americans, which is worth mentioning because the year was 1940, and the place was rural Florida. If you wanted to go any deeper into the racist South, you'd need a submarine. Celesta's mind didn't work that way, though. She spent her life being treated lousy for how her body looked, and she wasn't eager to transfer the bigotry to skin color.

Celesta had figured out how to thrive as a fat lady. But that didn't change the fact that her fat friends kept dying. Even when trying not to be fat. She and her sister-in-law had tried diet pills, and the only ones that worked appeared to have been mail-order military-grade methamphetamine. Both women lost weight. Her sister-in-law was quite svelte the day those pills blew out two valves of her heart and killed her. Dolly stopped taking them, barely in time to survive the kidney failure she'd thought was water retention.

Her mentor, Jolly Pearl, had well hidden the fact her carnival perch was a specially designed toilet she couldn't be moved from without help. Pearl had a heart attack and died while performing on a bright sunny day. She was buried in a rough wooden box, since no coffin could hold her, and she was driven to her grave on a flat-bottomed truck. Her death and demeaning burial were a trauma for Celesta.

When Celesta Geyer/Dolly Dimples/Madame Celeste was fifty and weighed 555 pounds, she also had a heart attack.

Her doctor told her she could diet, or she could die. Those were her choices.

Celesta believed him.

She lost 440 pounds in a little over a year, entering the *Guinness Book of World Records* for the feat. She didn't use diet pills, which terrified her. She didn't have surgery. She restricted herself to 800 calories a day.

It was horrible. She hurt, she felt starved, and she was depressed.

But she did it. And the depression lessened, the cravings were checked, and she did not gain the weight back. Ever.

Reams of scientific studies, as well as the personal experience of billions of women who have dieted, agree: that's not something very many people can do. Especially the "keep it off" part. But Celesta bucked the status quo once again.

Celesta, age fifty-seven, advertising her diet plan

No longer a viable circus fat lady, Celesta became a diet guru and talk-show celebrity, pitching a (sort of) sensible calorie-restriction diet. She died in 1982, at age eighty-one, at a reported 121 pounds.

Celesta didn't lose that weight to be sexy, popular, or even normal, since she'd made herself a life she loved as Dolly Dimples and Madame Celeste. She lost it because it was threatening to take away something she valued above all else.

Celesta Geyer loved LIFE. Not just "being alive"; any sad sack can manage that. She loved what life is made of: going places, doing hard things, navigating new people, being surprised, taking chances. She sacrificed and fought to keep all that. Fat *and* thin, Celesta Geyer honored life as few people can.

AIDA OVERTON WALKER

Maybe it was uncouth to tread the vaudeville stage,
and maybe it altered the bigotry of an entire age.

Aida knew how to dance. She knew how to merge discipline and grace in physical movement. The special thing about Aida is that she didn't use her abilities to move just her own body; she delicately took the hand of an entire nation and guided them to shift position.

It's a terrible misnomer to call anything you think will be easy "a cakewalk." Aida is the reason we have the term, and her journey was quite formidable.

Historians believe the dance originated among slaves. It was performed with the approval and enjoyment of slaveholders, despite being a flat-out mockery of those slaveholders. It was like saying, "See me dancing like I'm so arrogant that the stick wedged up my rear end is made of pure hard ivory? That's you. This is how you look. I am making fun of you." Slaveholders perhaps dwelt too far up inside their own rear ends to get the joke, and history is richer for it.

Aida had already made a name for herself on the vaudeville circuit when she joined the top-billed Black comedy duo Williams and Walker in the late 1880s. The duo wanted their finale to have the finest performance of the cakewalk New York had ever seen. Aida auditioned and proved she was the woman to provide it.

HOW TO CAKEWALK

The dance was a satire of ballroom dances, or "reels," where men and women lined up facing each other, and took turns dancing together down the human hallway made by other dancers. The dancing couple pretended to be two high-class people trying to impress each other with their elegance and style, doing a flourish-filled high-stepping promenade together.

She added class to Williams and Walker's very funny but otherwise pretty lowbrow vaudeville act. In fairness, it was sort of a requirement to be lowbrow if you were doing vaudeville. But that wasn't their endgame. Aida and her partners (one of whom, George, she married in 1899) were running the wires to detonate low racial stereotypes into high-art fireworks. How? For starters, Williams and Walker put on the best blackface minstrel show in the nation.

Minstrel shows were a vaudeville act containing songs, dancing, and the earliest innovation of standup comedy. That's all lovely. The peculiar part, or at least it was peculiar to Aida and her co-stars, was that it was traditionally done by white men in "burnt cork," or blackface, basing the humor on how befuddled and amoral Black people were. Williams and Walker *were* Black, and thus quite purposefully eliminated the middle (white) man.

George Walker explained, "We thought that as there seemed to be a great demand for black faces onstage, we would do all we could to get what we felt belonged to us by the laws of nature. Our bills attracted the attention of managers, and gradually we made our way in."

"Williams and Walker All the Rage in London"

They called their blackface act "Two Real Coons." It was shocking language. And it was genius. Not only did it draw a packed house; it also reminded the white audience, however subtly, that Black faces belonged to humans. Humans smart enough to take your money if you wanted the privilege of looking at them. One more stereotype turned upside down, and one more step in the complicated choreography of a society that needed change.

Aida was in the minstrel show to make the nudge even firmer. She added beauty and grace to the performance. To perhaps suggest there was incongruity in aligning this talented erudite lady with the term *coon*.

That's how you dance, of course. To lead your partner you apply gentle pressure, prods. People hate being shoved; but skillful nudges can make them voluntarily change where they're standing.

As I said, Aida knew how to dance.

Her male co-stars subverted expectation by being actual Black men. She subverted them by refusing to behave as audiences preferred to see Black women behave: insipid, angry, or hyper-sexual.

That wasn't Aida's style, though. She wouldn't "accidentally" show her polka-dotted underdrawers or chase anyone with a rolling pin. She sang and danced with skill; her personal style was modeled on the regal Gibson Girl look, one seldom seen on Black performers. With each performance she became more synonymous with the increasingly popular cakewalk.

Williams and Walker were playing the long game . . . and winning. When the trio's enormous vaudeville success had opened doors across America and in Europe for "colored" performers, they were finally famous and wealthy enough to do what they really wanted to do.

They wrote and performed the first successful musicals on Broadway with entirely Black casts. Their musicals were usually set in Africa, with Williams and Walker playing American yokels trying to interact with regal and highly civilized African characters.

Here was another careful push from a skillful lead: two Black men on the stage acting the goof so that fifty Black men and women could also be on stage portraying courtly dignity and decorum with precise English. That was important. In an era before mass communications showed there was more than one way to speak fluent American, formal oration with singular diction was a signifier of personal worth. It was one that a lot of folks didn't think Black people were capable of.

Aida choreographed and performed in the musicals. One, *In Dahomey* (1902–05), was so popular the cast gave a command performance for Edward VII and the British royal family at Buckingham Palace. It was a private showing because after the play, Aida taught the royals to cakewalk.

Now. Consider. The cakewalk was a satire of American "nobility," who themselves were doing their best to copy British nobility, who were led by the royals, who were *now paying Aida to teach them to mock themselves more efficiently in their own living room.* If you've ever been confused about the slippery definition of *irony*, this was what that is.

It's 1903, so she can't mic drop. Old-timey director bullhorn drop. Aida out.

When she arrived back in America, having taught Queen Alexandra how to do a precise kangaroo hippity hop, New York high society was waiting. Aida's reputation was so sterling, and her talent so revered, that the finest white families in New York were sending their daughters to attend Mrs. Walker's Cakewalk Instructionals at the Waldorf Astoria. That meant rich white girls lining up to learn how to be as graceful and as chic as a Black woman for, as far as I can tell, the first time in American history.

A sketch of Aida performing her Cakewalk Instructional

Aida's cakewalk was a new art form. She didn't let her students behave clownishly or make elaborate indelicate motions. A 1903 article described her style: No "shamble and strut" was allowed. Her cakewalk was "devoid of suggestiveness and coarseness." She banned the flailing of hankies. Only trash flail hankies. True ladies need only extend the wrist at a delicate angle to communicate everything that a lewd hanky did.

It's not certain that Aida was the first Black American to bring a dance craze into the social lives of white Americans, but most dance "crazes" before Aida involved being able to match your box step to a violin's tricky 3/4 tempo. And by the 1920s, pretty much all the cool dances originated from an African American source. (Well, maybe not the Macarena. Or Orange Justice. Do people still Vogue? It's moot. Those things are surely to be considered more cultural upheavals than dances.)

When her husband, George, died of syphilis in 1908, Aida continued acting in musicals with Williams, dressing in drag and doing her husband's parts. She kept hard at work toward her goal of revealing the abilities of Black performers to a reticent world.

By 1912, she had enough social and professional cred to play the lead in one of the only female-led performances (and the *only* acceptable sexual play) welcomed on the stages of polite pre-World War I society: *Salome,* at Oscar Hammerstein's Victoria Theatre, on Forty-second Street, New York City. The *New York Tribune* delicately announced the inherent risk in an article titled "Dusky Ragtime Champion to Challenge Art at Hammerstein's." The article read: "It is the first time that a dusky beauty has dared to brave ART [fully capitalized] in his lair along Broadway. But Mr. Hammerstein is convinced it can be done without serious consequences, either to him or the artist."

We must take it on faith that "dusky" was a 1912 compliment. I'm sure I'd have been flattered to be described as "a waxy enchantress" or "a bleachy nymph."

True to Aida's nature, her *Salome* was not the least bit tawdry. She didn't play to the grubby hoi polloi back in early vaudeville days, so she sure wasn't going to do it here. Her performance was sophistication merged with sensuality, and it was a great success. Proof? She topped Harry Houdini on the marquee. And they both topped "Don the Talking Dog." (Don't scoff. Even great actresses and magicians are a dime a dozen. How many talking dogs do you know?)

Oddly enough, the community Aida had most to pacify as a result of her "unladylike" profession was upper-class Black society. Her decision to use the stage to showcase her skill seemed risky to people at pains to prove they were not inherently inferior. She wrote often in Black periodicals, defending her work. In a 1905 editorial in *Colored American*, she predicted the future of racial integration when she stated, "Some of our so-called society people regard the Stage as a place to be ashamed of. . . . In this age we are all fighting the one problem—that is the color problem! I venture to think and dare to state that our profession does more toward the alleviation of color prejudice than any other profession among colored people."

History would prove her right. By the 1920s, American screens, stages, and recording studios were welcoming Black artists far in advance of other professions. Aida had pioneered yet another shift of position, urging forward a century full of incremental change.

Aida did not live to see the length of her legacy. Her dance was brilliant, but it was brief. She died of kidney disease in 1914, at the age of thirty-five.

Aida was a spectacle. She shocked the world by being delightful, modest, and talented in an era when nobody wanted to pay to see those virtues displayed by a Black woman on stage. She redefined what Americans might expect from a Black performer. Aida stood apart gracefully, and by doing so she drew people together.

THE CHERRY SISTERS

How terrible could they really be,
if people paid thousands to have a look-see?

At 10 p.m. on a chill night in November of 1896, the audience in New York City's Olympia Theater waited with high expectations.

They had come to see the Worst Vaudeville Act in the World: The Cherry Sisters. An act consisting of songs, costumes, poetry readings, a morality play with gypsies, and, they hoped, an astounding disregard for personal dignity or performative skill. They were not disappointed.

Under the headline "Four Freaks from Iowa," the *New York Times* described their act thus:

> Three lank figures and one short and thick walked awkwardly to the centre of the stage. They were all dressed in shapeless red gowns, made by themselves almost surely, and the fat sister carried a bass drum. They stood quietly for a moment. . . . Then

they began to sing, in thin strained soprano, and their song was of all the songs in the world . . . "Ta Ra rah boo de aye." People listened in amazement as one senseless verse followed another, accompanied at rare intervals by a graceless gesture and intermittent thumps on the big drum.

They then trundled off for a quick costume change. Addie needed a mustache and Effie a handkerchief to put on her head to perform their morality tale, written by Effie herself, "The Gypsy's Warning." (The plot of the skit is contained entirely within the title. There was a gypsy. Who warned.) The review continued: "The three sad, flat-chested sisters went through some dialogues which they thought to be dramatic. The words were borrowed from cheap story-papers, and the action from the poverty-stricken imagination of minds worn bare and hard by rough work done on meagre fare."

The reviewer said they were grotesque, but not grotesque enough to be interesting. He concluded, "It is sincerely hoped that nothing like them will ever be seen again."

That reviewer did not have his finger on the pulse of the vaudeville-viewing public. The fellow had just seen an early performance of what would become one of the top-grossing acts at the turn of the twentieth century. Their breasts might have been flat, but their commercial appeal was lusty, full, and heaving.

It was a sibling affair. Though that reviewer got the rare pleasure of viewing four Cherry Sisters, the act was usually just three—Addie, Effie, and Jessie. Back home on the farm in Iowa were two more sisters, and the sisters' whole act existed only because of one lost brother. He'd lit out for Chicago after their parents died, never to be heard from again. All five of his sisters put on a concert to raise money to try to find him, and they raised $100. That was a small fortune for the time and place! (The *time* being their pitiable hour of need and the *place* being the generous hearts of their small-town neighbors.)

*Effie, Lizzie, and Addie attempt a comeback
in 1929 with "The Gypsy's Warning"*

The young women had basically carried out a successful 1890s GoFundMe campaign, but that wasn't how they saw it. They'd packed the house! They'd entertained! They had an act! They promptly rented a bigger hall in a bigger town.

Thus began the Great Cherry Sisters Debate.

The question is not: Were they bad? Because they were. Unequivocally. Terrible. Stank like whale carcass. Rather, the world still wonders: Did they *know* they were bad?

The review of their next performance, in the *Cedar Rapids Gazette*, was already puzzling over the question: "they surely could not realize last night that they were making such fools of themselves. If some indefinable instinct of modesty could not have warned them that they were acting the part of monkeys, it does seem like the overshoes thrown at them would have conveyed the idea."

Were they actually brilliant, playing *audiences* for the fools in an absurdist performance art, where the joke is *You paid money and actually sat through this torment?* Or, were they so dim and stubborn that they truly believed they were good?

CHUTES AND ZOO. Every Afternoon and Evening.

The 3 Celebrated Cherry Sisters,

Most Original Performers on Earth, AND GREAT VAUDEVILLE SHOW.

CAKEWALK CONTEST TO-MORROW NIGHT.

Reserve Seats by Phone—Park 23.

Top Billing in 1900 San Francisco.
And look! A cakewalk!

If Effie's old gypsy lady could have broken the fourth wall, perhaps she'd have told us in a spooky voice that the answer lies in what the Cherry Sisters did offstage.

It was the same stuff they did while onstage, providing a rough but telling psychological profile.

Take the *Gazette* review. The Cherry Sisters said that it was some straight-up libelous malarkey. *Malarkey!* They went to the *Gazette* office and demanded a retraction. They filed a libel suit against the editor, Fred P. Davis. It was reported he'd been arrested! For the crime of being a big jerk!

But . . . then the Cherry Sisters agreed with the *Gazette* to hold the trial at the local theater, where Davis was sentenced to propose marriage to one of the sisters. Which means there was no actual trial, but there was a great deal of fuss and entertainment. Suggesting that, more than justice for their indignities, the Cherry Sisters wanted attention. They wanted to be part of the fun, even if the only way to be included was to be the butt of the joke.

Enforcing this theory, the *Gazette* eventually printed a retraction, but insisted the sisters write it themselves. Which they did, without use of dignity, dictionary, or the proofreading skills of a third grader—all of which were readily available.

> The Cherry Sisters Concert that appeared in the *Gazette* the other evening was initily a mistake and we take it back. The young ladies were refined and modist in every respict And their intertanement was as good as any that has been given in the city by home people.

The Cherry Sisters filed a lot of frivolous lawsuits during their lifetimes, a habit associated with the attention-starved. Usually for small offenses: a thug took their money from a theatre manager before they could get it, Effie's finger got smashed in the door when she was trying to shove a rude man out—things like that.

Their biggest court case was when they sued a nasty fellow who was doing pieces for Iowa's *Odebolt Chronicle*. He had written: "Their long skinny arms equipped with talons at the extremities, swung mechanically, and soon were waved frantically at the suffering audience. Their mouths opened like caverns, and sounds like the wailing of damned souls issued therefrom."

Skinny? *Skinny?* Oh, those were fightin' words for farm girls in the 1890s.

If their suit against Mr. Davis had been a farce, the defamation suit against the *Odebolt Chronicle* was for real. It went clear to the Iowa Supreme Court, which ruled that newspapers have the right to freely criticize public performances, even in a downright rude and ungentlemanly fashion.

Between all these lawsuits, the Cherry Sisters kept getting booked at vaudeville venues in small towns. They performed the same act for the unruly audiences, and they kept getting "cigars, cigarettes, rubbers" thrown at them. (Back then, "rubbers" meant "rainboots." I hope. I sincerely hope.)

And they kept getting paid by sold-out audiences.

In interviews, they answered that ever-present question. They said, "We are not bad." They explained that the claim they often performed behind a chicken-wire cage to protect themselves again projectiles was pure media nonsense. Nasty reviewers didn't bother to mention the sisters' thousands of entertained fans. If things got thrown, it was usually only by two or three ruffians. And that time Jessie ran on stage brandishing a gun, in front of 200 witnesses, and got pelted with turnips—that never even happened! That's some more malarkey right there, and they'd sue you but good for that if the State Supreme Court hadn't already said they couldn't.

The sisters mostly retired their act after Jessie died in 1903 from typhus. Effie and Addie performed sporadically over the next couple of decades. Sometimes their sister Lizzie filled in, but they never tainted their classic routine with any major updates or improvements. People still came, but fewer now; the ferocious vibe of experiencing something outrageous had cooled. It just wasn't as much fun to throw vegetables at middle-aged aunties.

Offstage, the Cherry Sisters still wanted to be noticed, even if it was with disdain. Effie had two (failed) runs for mayor of Cedar Rapids.

American journalist and historian Jack El-Hai, in his essay "Shaming the Cherry Sisters," points out that Effie's campaign was designed to annoy. "[Effie] laid out her platform, which included such unpopular initiatives as a 9 p.m. winter curfew for adults, closing public parks to eliminate them as

Addie and Effie still gloriously grotesque in their golden years

trysting spots for the young, requiring swimmers to use more modest bathing suits, and the outlawing of profanity on the street." El-Hai notes the parallel: "It was the old formula of annoying the public in exchange for their attention."

After the vaudeville, the revival, the lawsuits, and the goofball politics were exhausted, the Cherry Sisters finally ran out of ways to perform. They faded away. Having no money left from their years of successful anti-popularity, they spent their old age in the state's care. Between 1933 and 1944, all the remaining Cherry Sisters died.

Did they know they were bad? Of course. And they knew being bad was good. That's no different from a literal million young people acting outrageously on their social media accounts for "likes."

The unladylike thing about the Cherry Sisters wasn't their off-key singing or stubborn egos. It's that they didn't care the attention they were getting was negative. Their lack of dignity wasn't in being in vaudeville and in getting harassed; it was that uncomfortable fact that they sought negative attention and liked it. Don't pity them; that would be insulting a conscious choice. Because the turnips were coming at these impoverished farm girls, one way or another.

The Cherry Sisters took control of how they arrived; they preferred to take those turnips hurled onto a stage instead of breaking their backs to squat down and pull them, with their own hands, from the frozen earth. That sort of agency deserves a round of applause.

2.

BALLBUSTERS

**BUSINESS BROADS
WHO PLAYED WITH THE BIG BOYS**

I t was hard to be a businesswoman in the old days. Especially since science tells us that women didn't become actual people until sometime in the late 1970s. They tried, though.

In 1906, one Caroline A. Huling wrote "Letters of a Business Woman to her Niece," a manual to help women counteract their unfortunate femininity in a business setting. Here are some of her tips:

DON'T SPEAK IN A LISTLESS VOICE. (Filing and collating is *fun*. Act like it!)

DON'T TRY TO BE MANNISH EITHER IN DRESS OR IN MANNER. (She also denigrates dressing girly. You might wonder, then, what does that leave? Ho ho! Keep wondering, for there will be many a riddle to solve if you wish to pass this way.)

DON'T COMPLAIN OF YOUR HEALTH . . . *keep silent about your ailments and you will gain more sympathy and admiration by your courage than by any amount of groaning.* (Your employers regard "headache," "flu," and "cancer" as synonyms for "menstruation," and they really just . . . just don't want to hear about it.)

It was a difficult balance to strike—how to make money after the masculine fashion, while maintaining socially appropriate femininity.

So difficult, in fact, that at least three successful businesswomen refused to even try. They dressed slovenly, complained loudly, avoided men unless it was profitable to use them, and occasionally drew guns on fellas who just wouldn't get with the program. And they all made a killing.

HETTY GREEN

Self-made billionaire,
ain't even gonna pretend to care.

S uppose you find yourself a finance genius in the mid-nineteenth century. And lo, you also find yourself with a vagina.

What is the proper way to integrate these two contradictory elements?

A wise woman might marry well. She might, with a meek, submissive manner, gently guide her husband with passive observations during dinner: "I do believe I heard Lady Babsycock say that her son would be selling all their land to avoid that dastardly new rail line being laid. Such a shame; they were going to have a lovely summer cottage by the river. . . .You know, the one where all those large industrial barges load and unload their cargo? It's good they're selling . . . someone will come along and build an enormous town there any moment. More figgy mince quail, my love?"

There were doubtless many women who took this route successfully.

And then, there was Hetty, the Witch of Wall Street. Hetty Green who, in the late nineteenth and early twentieth centuries, was the richest self-made woman in the world.

She became a billionaire (by today's dollars) with her stunning Wall Street investment strategies at a time when a woman needed her husband's permission to open so much as a savings account. She was eccentric to the point of being bizarre; she was a miser, a hoarder, a questionable mother, and a terrifying wife.

And she was *brilliant*.

Hetty wanted money. She was good at getting it. She didn't want to spend or share it. And she didn't care one copper cent what you thought about that. That last bit—her unfeminine apathy toward her public persona—was Hetty's greatest social transgression.

One of the reasons the Witch of Wall Street was disliked in her time (the *W* in "Witch" was pronounced with a hard *B* by the many men she worked among) was because she did not stay within the "feminine sphere"—a popular nineteenth-century term to describe a woman's place in society. Rather, Hetty stomped through the female sphere, left muddy boot prints across the male sphere, and made herself at home in a jagged little cube with the words "Property of Hetty: SCRAM" scrawled on the side.

Hetty's particular talent was *contrarian investing*, a useful skill when an economy keeps collapsing (as America's did, on average, every twenty years of Hetty's long life). It's not a terribly friendly way to make money—especially

ON THE CONTRARY

Contrarian investing is when you buy things that everyone else thinks valueless, and then sit on them until they are valuable again. Like buying a lot of a railroad's stock after a train from that particular railroad crashed into an orphanage. The stock would plummet from unpopularity, but Hetty would have been *all over* "KidSmash R&R." She would have known that only KidSmash R&R had the rights to build a bridge over an increasingly valuable river crossing. It might have taken a few years for the company to atone enough to be allowed to build it, but Hetty was patient.

for women, who were taught not to be contrary about anything.

But we can't assign Hetty's strange place in history to unfair sexism alone. That would be cheating. She was far more complicated and she deserves a more intimate look.

Hetty was a Quaker, and when she finally deigned to give interviews in her later years, she attributed much of her "odd" ways to the pillars of simple, plain living the Quaker faith espouses. And okay, that could explain the shabby clothes; and eating broken graham crackers and dry oatmeal every day; insisting that the banks in which she invested provide her free office space daily to conduct her personal business; constantly moving around to cheap apartments and refusing to pay for heating them, even when her children were with her; declining to pay $150 for hernia surgery and instead keeping the bulge of her torn muscle in place with a stick wedged between her thighs; or not paying for her teenage son's medical care after he was run down by a small carriage in the street until he had to have an amputation, which she also did not pay for.

There was the thornier question of how much a person of overwhelming wealth and religious conviction is expected to give to charity. One hundred years after her death, a few deep-diving biographers discovered some contributions she made to schools and old-folks' homes. Not big contributions, but still. We could say, "There. End of controversy. She didn't make fanfare about her contributions is all!"

It's just . . . that time when her aunt died and she left $2 million to charity instead of Hetty? And Hetty challenged the will in court? Then produced the most painfully obvious forgery of her aunt's will, declaring Hetty was to get everything? She did not succeed, but I think we should take a moment and be impressed that she even thought to try! That's some serious moxie, right there!

So, with Hetty Green, as with all real humans in history, we have to balance a sober yin with a raging yang. She personally nursed her ex-husband attentively on his deathbed, but she tried to cure her son's infected, smashed leg with vegetable oil and a tidy dose of "Stop whining, Ned." (To be fair, the medical practice of the era wasn't sterling—that leg was probably coming off, one way or another.)

Sylvia and her mother, Hetty Green, on the joyous . . .
well, acceptable . . . tolerable . . . my God, you are a constant
disappointment like everyone else in this sin-stained world . . .
occasion of Sylvia's wedding

She gave her daughter a nice wedding, but that was after years of making her sleep on the floor in random cold apartments as a deterrent against robbers or tax collectors—who were, of course, the same thing to Hetty. (And really, it was highly unsportsmanlike of the U.S. government to all of a sudden in 1913 impose a yearly income tax on people. Did you know we didn't use to have income tax? Hetty sure did!) And I'm not saying it was Hetty's intention to literally throw her daughter in their path to expedite her own escape . . . probably. She did sleep with that revolver tied to her wrist. But where else would you tie it, really?

It was one of her many eccentricities that anyone might develop when bearing up under staggering wealth. Like taking wily and convoluted walks to work to throw off possible kidnappers. Especially after her children were too large to throw.

Hetty died in 1916. Her son, one-legged Ned, was now rich beyond the dreams of avarice, because Hetty did not leave an observable amount of her billions to charity. Ned enjoyed freedom and wealth throughout the roaring '20s, married his favorite prostitute, and built the biggest yacht then known—though it turned out he got seasick and never sailed on it.

His sister, Sylvia, retired to peaceful obscurity. Like her brother, she had no children. She inherited his money after his death, as well.

At the time of her own death in the 1950s, Sylvia was not a billionaire. In today's money she was worth only around $100 million. Her will, found crumpled in an old desk and uncontested, left her mother's remaining fortune to sixty-three different charities and educational institutions. Many consider this karma—that after a lifetime spent trying to keep her money all to herself, it should end up in the hands of the charities she'd shunned in life.

But why should Hetty need cosmic punishment for doing what she was born to do, the way she wanted to do it? Should Hetty have been nicer, more generous, more maternal? She could have been. But then she wouldn't have had the elements in her that drove her to be *Hetty*. That singularity of purpose, that fierce fixation, the ruthlessness that makes humans break from set roles and do hard things. Never mind leaving a will. Ferocity was Hetty's legacy, uncontested.

Poker Alice

POKER ALICE STUBBS

Hard livin' lady,
and it ain't your business if hers was a little shady.

The Wild West was for men. It's even hidden in the term you learned in seventh-grade history class: (Man)ifest Destiny. They didn't do that on purpose, but nonetheless there it is.

From Deadwood to Dodge City, wild men of any ethnicity, be it Native, Mexican, Black, and of course just scads of white, had the opportunity to booze, rob, fight, shoot, gamble, and whore. The only law was what you could get away with without being shot.

Evidence exists that women did not enjoy that lawless freedom nearly as much. "Good" migrant women were required to abandon their homes and follow their men, shoulders stooped with the responsibility of civilizing those places of filth and desolation, heads buried in enormous bonnets that prevented flirtatious side-glancing and, like blinkers on the oxen whose feces they were obliged to cook their food upon, kept them from seeing something that might spook them.

"Bad" women almost exclusively took up sex work, which was unsafe and often involuntary.

But what about a woman who was neither good nor bad? What about a woman who was born to be just as wild as the men, and on her own terms? What about Alice?

The facts of any story about Poker Alice's life will be both thin and heavily padded—a paradox absolutely necessary to make a legend.

For (almost) certain, we know these things about Alice. She married a mining engineer and moved to a Colorado boomtown. They were called "boomtowns" because the discovery of precious metals initiated quick population growth. In Alice's case, the moniker is far more unfortunate: her first husband died in a mine explosion.

Left on her own, Alice didn't go home to her family, which might or might not have existed; she did not (probably?) become a prostitute; and she said she tried to be a schoolteacher, but honestly, no one's buying that. What she *did* do was start playing cards for money.

Exceedingly well. "Resting bitchface" isn't an insult if you do it so well men literally fold under the strength of it.

For fifteen years, Alice roamed the West independently, not as a woman pressed into the service of men, like most of her female contemporaries but, rather, because she *loved* the lifestyle. She was perpetually on the hunt for gamblers skilled or foolish enough to compete with her.

She said, "I . . . never stayed long at any [one place]. There were too many other games to buck, too many chances

THE FACTS (PROBABLY)

Name: Alice Ivers Duffield Tubbs Huckert Tubbs

Birthplace: England. Unless Ireland. One census says Ohio. Might have been Virginia. (What're you, a cop?)

Age: Born in Eighteen-fifty-furrmityfrimm

Marital Status: All. Except when none.

Children: Seven. None. Possibly two. There was definitely a cat.

Vice Crimes Committed: Yes!

Men Killed: One. That *you* know about.

Profession: High-stakes gamer, national treasure, last of the Old West baddies

for big winning, too many camps waiting to be invaded. The life of a gambler was a life of travel, the constant excitement of something new."

Sure, Alice suffered the delusion that it was no one's business if she chose to live a life without the womanly virtues of chastity, temperance, and not shooting at people. Maybe she didn't understand that *excitement* is just a complicated pronunciation of the word *sin*. But she lived that delusion so well, no one ever tried to dissuade her.

In mining towns, distractions were more valuable than the gold those lonely men tried to pull from the earth. Saloons hired the few women who drifted through their backwaters to deal cards, vying over the most entertaining hostesses. Alice was peerless as a dealer *and* as a player. She commanded a $25 paycheck from any establishment she dealt for (that was a lot for a gal back then). She'd work the graveyard shift, since no husband or pimp demanded she be anywhere else. Then, she'd clock out, switch sides of the table, and win back some of the house's money she'd just collected.

The night she realized her true calling was when she was in Silver City, New Mexico, in the early 1890s. She had newly procured a second (and favorite) husband, Warren Tubbs. Warren was a housepainter who, she recalled, "thought he was a gambler." Bless his heart. He soon learned to step back and let Alice do her thing.

She broke the house's bank by winning $900 that night. So, she swirled the faro board around, announced *herself* as the new bank, and told the men to place their bets. Alice recalled, "The word spread that a fool woman had taken off the limit and was willing to buck the entire town, and soon everyone in the mining camp of Silver City who possessed a gambling instinct had become arrayed against me."

Alice recreating her glory days
for a 1920s newspaper profile

She left with $6,000 (around $165,000 today) that night.

Alice did not invest her frequent windfalls sensibly. Why? Because go to hell, that's why. She lit out to New York City whenever she won big, buying fine dresses and staying at the most swank of hotels. When the money ran out, she'd return to the chaos and dust of the lawless mining towns.

Alice and Warren traveled the boomtowns until around 1900, when they settled down on a ranch outside

Deadwood. They had a quiet time there. Maybe. Some papers said they had seven children that decade! Which would have been quite a feat under any circumstances. But considering Alice would have been nearly fifty at the start of the twentieth century, it's likely one of her many embellishments.

Her husband, Warren, died in 1910. Alice wanted to go back to Deadwood, but the town was trying to make itself respectable, and so it gave her the bum's rush. She bought a house in Sturgis, South Dakota, to live in. With six young . . . well, let's say "roommates," who also happened to be professional prostitutes. Coincidences happen; you can't prove *anything* and what's it to you, anyway? Her home was a convenient walking distance from Fort Meade, and the many soldiers therein named it "Poker's Palace." Which I believe was homage to a seventeenth-century French château of some cultural renown that likely maybe existed and was called Poque d'Paleis. Probably nuns lived there. What? (It's impossible to prove a negative, you know.)

Alas, the Old West was dissipating under Alice's feet, and her effort to maintain it was ill-fated. In the waning years of her life, Alice told reporters that she only ever drew her .38 pistol twice. She usually left out the time she shot the repeating rifle.

In 1913, there was a scuffle among the guests at Poker Palace. The power was cut off, and Alice shot a rifle in the dark. When the lights came back on, a calvaryman was dead. The courts determined that Alice had shot in self-defense, so no charges were filed. She *was* found guilty of keeping a house of ill repute, though. Sentencing was not enforced, but as we shall see, neither was it forgotten.

After the shootout, Alice had to let the Wild West go. Men went off to World War I, and they came back to Prohibition. She married a third time, but she wasn't that into it, living apart and retaking Tubbs's name after her third husband's 1924 death. Soon she found herself living alone in a small house in Sturgis, flat broke. Alice had outlived the Old West.

In the mid-1920s, a nostalgia for the old days and the long-dead outlaws referred to as the "'76 Crowd" brought renewed interest in Poker Alice. She was, after all, the last of them. Buffalo Bill, Annie Oakley, Jesse James, Bat Masterson—they were all gone. Alice became popular again.

She was popular enough that, in 1928, the sheriff was called to raid a raucous party at Alice's home, where they found a great deal of illegal booze. Now in her seventies, she was arrested, pled guilty to drunkenness, and served thirty days in jail. A new State Attorney dug up the old case against her for running a brothel, and pulled the remarkably sleazy move of getting her sentenced to six months in prison for a crime that took place fifteen years earlier *and* in a completely different world.

"Oh, *hell* no," said the denizens of the Black Hills! Put Poker Alice in the state pen for being Poker Alice? Would you tell a drunken, wizened stogie-chomping cranky old crow not to fly? Hundreds signed a petition to see her pardoned, claiming her too old and too precious to survive prison.

Alice receives her governor's pardon

Alice went to the state capital to meet the governor of South Dakota to ask for a personal pardon. With a hot water bottle full of illegal whiskey hanging by a string around her neck. At her hotel, the evening before, she demanded the finest treatment, as she would have enjoyed in her glory days in New York. It was no small effort to sober her up the next morning to meet the governor.

She met the governor and told him to turn her loose so she could go back to her cat, named "Calamity Jane" after an old acquaintance.

So he did.

Alice died in 1930. Many memorials of her colorful life appeared, seeking to make her 150-proof high-octane life a more pleasant libation. It was mostly after her death that she became religious, generous, maternal, and kind-spirited. We don't know if she was any of those things.

But she didn't need to be any of those things. She needed the thrill of being alive and wild, in a time when and place where a woman living only for their own selves was committing a greater sin than prostitution, gambling, or killing, all put together. Poker Alice was here only to be fierce, independent, and sly. And she hit the jackpot.

REINDEER MARY ANTISARLOOK

Warm heart, cold hands—
owned the most powerful empire in the arctic lands.

R eindeer Mary was Alaska's first self-made lady millionaire. She did this without gold or cash, and while deflecting the attentions of countless men who wanted to "help" her manage her wealth. How did she achieve success? Well, Mary understood the importance of timing. So, she will appear in this, her own story, on her own schedule. Don't rush her.

Let us first discuss geography, and how it will kill you.

To understand how Mary became the richest woman in a land that routinely belched gold along random riverbeds, without ever touching a single flake herself, we first must understand that land. Which we can't, of course. We have pet robots that clean our floors and feel personally offended when a soda brand updates its logo. We best just stay humble in our opinions about nineteenth-century Alaska.

We can understand this much: Alaska is so cold.

The thousands of gold seekers who rushed to the subarctic shores weren't concerned about a bit of frost. They should have been, bless them, but they were not. Adventurers are used to living off the land. And "subarctic tundra" is technically a legitimate land designation!

Alaska offered this:

FOOD? Not without a terribly specialized hunter-gatherer skill set. We do have this ice, however.

PROTECTION FROM THE ELEMENTS? You can try! With your adorable canvas tent and little wool hat. Solid effort! You're going to freeze to death here. See the ice?

TRANSPORTATION? Oh, gosh no. Snow *hates* it when you try to move around in it. Have you tried maybe sliding on the ice? Because, there *is* plenty of ice.

DEATH? Even if your shoulders are stooped from the sacks of gold? Yes! Most assuredly. Buried in ice!

Now we shall talk about zoology, and how *not* knowing about it can kill you. (Don't rush Mary! She'll appear when she's ready.)

The thing about reindeer is that they are magical. Santa could have chosen moose, or elk, or gone to the other end of the planet and had twelve dapper little penguins pull his sleigh. But reindeer, now that's practical magic.

WHY REINDEER ARE MAGIC

- Can haul 200 pounds of cargo, plus sleigh, through any depth of snow.

- Can travel about ten miles an hour, up to a hundred miles a day.

- Eat little—a main part of their diet is prolific moss, which thrives in Arctic conditions.

- Taste delicious.

- Have sinew that makes nylon-strength rope.

- Have hides that protect against subarctic temperatures.

- Can breed quick and reliably.

- Can be milked for a delightful cheese.

If only Alaska . . . had any reindeer.

Fifty miles across the Bering Strait, in Russia, the Siberian Chukchi tribes had reindeer. But despite being genetic cousins to the Yupik and Inuit tribes (which were collectively called "Eskimos" in colloquial 1890s English) of North America, they didn't like each other. And they didn't share reindeer.

Now we shall talk about politics, which is honestly pretty indifferent about whether you live or die. Here, let me speed it up. The U.S. government looked at its newly acquired 665,000 square miles of frozen deathscape and said, "Our Natives ought to also have reindeer." So, they bought some from Russia, brought in "Laplanders" from Scandinavia to teach herding, and slowly distributed the reindeer to the Native population.

The Natives would pay "rent" to the government measured in reindeer head, but they could keep any surplus reindeer for themselves. This arrangement was intended to widen the Native population's ability to provide for themselves while enriching the government.

Mary thought it was a fine idea. She would know; she grew up off the shores of Alaska, on a trading post on the island of St. Michael. She was the daughter of a Native woman and an unknown Russian trapper and was proficient in Native languages as well as English and Russian. She and her husband, Charlie Antisarlook, acted as translators for the Alaska Territory during this reindeer exchange. (See, Mary was here all along. She already knew everything she needed to know about geography, zoology, and politics; she was just waiting for us to catch up.)

Mary helped procure the animals from the Chukchi people in Russia and spread word among the Natives of the government's intentions. Which were too slow, even for Mary's patience. When two years passed and only the white-run religious missions and government outposts were receiving the herds, it was Mary who called out the government shenanigans. Or, as one official wrote, "Mary—that half breed Russian wife—is stirring up trouble among the natives."

Oh, yes she was! Thus in 1895, Mary and Charlie Antisarlook were the first Native Alaskans to be "loaned" 120 reindeer from the U.S. government. That could have made for a happy ending right there. But literally months later, in 1896, gold was discovered in the Yukon.

BOOM.

Nome, Alaska, 1900. Some of the 20,000 men
who made up the Nome gold rush.

They came: the thousands of unprepared, hungry gold seekers. So many would pass through Nome. And most of them came to Mary for help.

Luckily she was just as proficient in handling men as she was handling reindeer. Charlie and Mary were excellent reindeer ranchers. Within three years they were keeping more reindeer than they were paying back to the government. Unfortunately, in 1900, Charlie and two of his brothers died in a measles epidemic.

Charlie's surviving brothers approached Mary and reminded her: Inuit tradition means that everything she and Charlie had built now belonged to them. Traditionally, a widow was cared for by her in-laws and the extent of their charity.

Mary wasn't up for that.

She had been the one to build the reindeer enterprise from the ground up. No inheritance of this size or in this business had ever been up for grabs. She took her brothers-in-law to the Territory Court and the court ruled that, under white men's law, the widow inherits her husband's estate. Tradition isn't always to be venerated; in Mary's case, that tradition was unfair and impractical.

Now Mary had 400 head of reindeer, making her the richest woman in Alaska and the most powerful individual herder in the area.

Most Inuit women never ran the business end of the herding—another tradition Mary didn't see the sense in. She controlled all aspects of her business. She employed women to render the reindeer for their many uses. Mary also ran an apprentice program for young herdsmen. She sold meat to the gold prospectors and even to the government to feed its soldiers. Not to mention the $100 a month she charged the army to use her deer for transportation.

Her animals were constantly poached by hungry men, so the government encouraged her to move her herd north to the Teller Reindeer Station, a government-run area that would offer protection. Mary thanked the government for their consideration and took the whole operation south.

Mary didn't need men, guns, or "civilization." She was a Native Alaskan woman. The icy wilderness that all but promised death to most newcomers was her home, and its dangers were her protection. Her herd just grew in size.

Aside from in-laws and lawmakers, there was one more sort of man Mary had to handle. These were the men who swarmed around the wealthy widow, with the intention of poaching her, not for her meat but for her money. They dogged her when she went to the village, flinging shameless woo.

White men's laws might help a widow, but they did squat-diddly for a married woman. Mary knew she'd legally forfeit her herd and wealth to whomever she married. When she did decide to remarry, it was in her own good time, to a nice fellow named Andrewuk, who didn't care about business or reindeer.

Mary had a business acumen that exceeded all her male counterparts. But that wasn't all she had. Having never borne any biological children, she began catching up and keeping all those who'd been left orphaned as a result of the sicknesses that the gold rush had brought to Alaska. She kept, at different times during the height of her wealth, between five and fifteen children in her home, all reaching maturity while feeling warm, fed, and loved. Her boys were brought up to be shepherds, her girls became excellent artisans working with reindeer hide.

Eventually, the gold rush ended, as did the demand for reindeer. By the time the Great Depression hit, Mary was poor again—or rather, back where she started.

For Mary, that was just fine. Meat had not been her only investment. Though both she and Hetty Green (see page 43) were business magnates, one of the reasons Mary was poor again had been her endless generosity. "No one is turned away from Reindeer Mary's house" was the refrain expressed throughout the territory.

"Sinrok Mary, the Reindeer Queen of Alaska," is her title. Half Russian, half Eskimo, she has gained wealth by her own business ability. Her life is a curious record of shrewd bargains and humane deeds

Newspaper profile of Mary from 1918

Mary died in 1948. When interviewed many years later as old ladies themselves, her granddaughters didn't talk of reindeer. They talked of Grandma's pretty face, her dancing at potlucks, and how her lap always had room for at least two children to sit.

Though she didn't stay there forever, Mary had found a niche in the world that only she could fill. She entered that niche when it was profitable and let go of it gracefully when it was no longer so. She wouldn't be ignored, but she was wise enough to ignore poor advice and flattery. Most of all, she knew her Alaskan Territory, and cared about the people who inhabited it. Any successful queen would do the same.

3.

THAT'S SISSY STUFF

DAMES WHO TOOK A PERFECTLY GOOD THING AND MADE IT BETTER

At the turn of the twentieth century, the clothing industry, journalism, and industrial engineering were all doing just fine, thank you very much. Men designed lovely, unaffordable, unwashable clothing for women with acceptable bodies. Newspapers were tiny, inky little fact sheets about railroad lines, bribes, and weekly cow prices. Industrial engineering was emerging as a sound method to get optimal performance from your workforce—a vast improvement over the traditional method of shooting guns into crowds of strikers (we'll learn more about that motivational ethos later!). Everything was fine. Couldn't be better.

Into this utopia came three women: an immigrant single mother, an attention-starved failed actress, and a mousy, over-educated baby factory. And they said, "But what if we . . . *tweaked* things a bit, gentlemen? Perhaps if we accessed the feminine mind in these areas, we might succeed (sell) more?"

Well, you know what happens to women who make a scene. They irritate everyone, are rejected flat out, and then change the world forever to fit the standard they designed because it's far more effective.

Same old story. At least for these ladies.

LENA HIMMELSTEIN
BRYANT MALSIN

Knocked up or fat?
Lena's got the goods to help with that.

Y ou know what was gross in 1900s New York City? Besides the open sewers and the rancid air and the street feces?

I'm talking *really* gross. Offensive. You know what was absolutely untenable to a turn-of-the-twentieth-century New Yorker?

Big, fat pregnant ladies.

Ugh! Look at them, bellies full of carnal sin, waddling about like a mobile advertisement for sperm. Eew. Eew!

You know what's even more gross? Ladies who had big bellies, or boobs, or booties, even when they're not pregnant. Fat chicks! Out in public! Like they think they're people! At least our sweet Celesta Geyer (see page 11) had the decency to join a circus. Luckily, since suitable clothing was scarce for a woman in any state of fleshy pulchritude, they were more likely to keep their bulbous-osity at home, where it belonged.

This is the world a sixteen-year-old immigrant named Lena stepped into, after fleeing Czarist Lithuania in 1895. And that's the world she would change, eliminating two different ways society kept women depressed, oppressed, and homebound. How did she free a century of women from that debilitating stigma?

Discreet use of pleats.

Lena, born in 1877, arrived in America unable to speak English. For our purposes, it's important to note that neither could she sew. But having just escaped a regime that was seeking to exterminate the rights of women, Jews, and the poor (Lena was all three), she was extremely adept at thriving in difficult situations. She was hired by a New York City dress boutique, and in four years of work she had mastered English, sewing, and social networking; so sublimely that her wages had risen from $1 a week to $15.

Her success also included finding a husband she loved: a jeweler named David Bryant. She married, left the dress shop, and settled down.

For a minute.

She delivered their first baby just months before David died of pneumonia. Lena was twenty years old, unemployed, a Jewish immigrant widow, and with a baby on her breast. She owned nothing but a pair of diamond earrings her husband had given her at their wedding. Playing by 1900 New York rules, that girl was doomed for the poorhouse.

Luckily, she wasn't playing by those rules. And she had

more than a pair of earrings. She had self-taught skills, all the connections she'd built through her conscientious professional behavior, and a fierce instinct for survival.

Lena pawned the earrings and bought her own sewing machine. She began working out of her small apartment, tapping the wealthy clientele she'd met as a shopgirl—clients who recognized and would pay for her talents.

She did everything herself. She designed their one-of-a-kind but still on-trend dresses, bought the expensive fabric, sewed the clothes to a flawless fit, then shucked on her coat and delivered the perfectly pressed creation to the lady's home, awkwardly waiting in the service entrance with her baby on her hip for payment so she could buy the fabric for her next job.

It was good for Lena that those rich wives of early twentieth-century New Yorkers were well-fed, bored, and possibly as a result, pregnant *a lot*. Lena herself confided that no "nice" woman of the day would be seen on the street in a noticeably expectant state. Nice ladies would go into "confinement," staying home.

Yet these women of the new century pushed boundaries that their Victorian mothers hadn't dared to. Confinement was so *boring*. If they made an effort to hide their shame, they reasoned, could they at least have friends over to their house?

We don't know the name of the first woman to whisper to young Lena that she needed a gown to disguise her pregnancy, but let's spill some bean dip on our distended baby bumps and powerful size 44DDs in her honor. Which, let's be honest, we were probably going to do anyway.

This anonymous woman's request for a little more bodily autonomy, a little freedom to keep being a human even as she gestated a new one, changed the world.

Lena created for this client, and then patented, her Maternity Dress #5. It was a tea gown, loose and flowing, elastic

at the waist, with a densely pleated skirt and a bodice layered with lace. Lena had made the first commercial maternity dress.

The dress was a *smash*. Friends sent friends to "the little Lithuanian widow" to procure a few more months of social freedom while *enceinte*. Lena did so well that in 1907, with the help of a small bank loan, she opened her own dress shop. She was nervous, and she transposed the letters of her name on the bank's paperwork. The money order came to her addressed to Lane Bryant.

Lena liked the sound of that name, and she kept it. Now Lena had a storefront and a product in high demand. The next step was to tell the world. Unfortu-

Lane Bryant "Maternity Dress #5,"
light blue with lace

nately, her product was simply too offensive to advertise.

It wasn't until 1911 that New York newspapers permitted Lane Bryant to buy a whole ad bearing the positively obscene words *Maternity Dress*. Apparently, the fellows who ran the advertising department had considered that phrase the 1911 equivalent of a high-definition photo of a raw placenta with attached umbilical cord snaking up into a stretched post-labor vaginal canal.

> **Maternity Dress:** (Patent Pending) **self adjusting, made in one piece.**
> Lane Bryant's new invention combines style and comfort. Can be worn through the entire period, and later, without the need of moving even one hook, and conceals absolutely all effects of a MATERNITY DRESS.
> FOULARD, CREPE DE CHINE, MULL, MARQUISETTE AND SWISS
> *Formerly $18.50 to $75.00* **14.75 to 49.50**

Which apparently moved product! Her entire stock was sold out the next day.

Lena's special talent in dressmaking went public at a perfect time. Women were becoming quite truculent in this new century, refusing to starve off their baby weight. It wasn't easy to stay bony in an era that had plentiful food and little physical labor. Especially with the corset having gone out of style and fashions becoming quite close-fitting. Women now sought clothes to flatter their figures, newly revealed by slimline skirts and fitted shirtwaists.

Lena designed.

By then, Lena had married an engineer named Albert Malsin. Lena hated "business," despite how good she was at it. "I have never liked to have anything to do with money," she reminisced in 1948. "I just liked to work at the thing that pleased me and then if others liked my designs, it made me happy to share my creations." She happily handed the business part of Lane Bryant to her husband. Credit where credit was due, Albert was as good at business as Lena was at design.

Women flocked to Lane Bryant for fashionable "odd size" clothing. (That meant "plus size" in the vernacular of the day.) It might seem a bit harsh to call the larger lady "odd," but it was significantly nicer than the title most people mentally assigned larger fashions, which ran along the lines of "Big Mama Duds for Tubbsy McWidebottoms."

Albert applied his engineering knowledge to fit Lena's clients. According to Carmen Nicole Keist, in her Ph.D. dissertation "The New Costumes of Odd Sizes" (2012), "Bryant and Malsin used statistical information from two hundred thousand women as well as personally measuring forty-five hundred of their customers to determine three general types of plus sized women."

Before Lane Bryant, "straight"-sized clothing was made larger by adding an extra two inches of fabric to the waist, the sleeves, the neck, and the hem. But women evolutionarily fortunate enough to have a surplus of fat often store their supply in different places. If you just kept adding two extra inches to accommodate a round belly, the sleeves would hang like elephant trunks and the neckline would highlight the curvaceous-ity of the belly button. New engineering was required.

Or, as Albert said in a 1915 edition of *Women's Wear Daily*, "The stout woman's body did not conform to the mathematical and logical grade rules. Her body was irrational, outside of the norm, and in the eyes of clothing manufacturers, in need of rationalization and correction."

Not conforming, illogical, irrational, outside the norm, in need of correction. You know what this means?

Fat chicks were punk before it was cool.

But . . . not all of them wanted to look it. So, Lena began designing dresses to "camouflage" those larger figures. They began selling her clothing by mail, which was private, far reaching, and extremely successful.

In 1916, Lane Bryant became one of the first multi-floor luxury department stores in New York City. That's also the year the company's sales exceeded $1 million (around $25 million in today's dollars). When the 1920s Lindy-Hopped its way into fashion, demanding women be shaped like teen-age boys, sales to "the stout" began to exceed the sales of the original maternity wear.

Lena's belief in giving people dignity extended beyond clothes, however. By the 1950s, according to the American Jewish History Society, "The more than 3,500 Lane Bryant employees participated in profit sharing, pension, disability, group life insurance plans, and fully reimbursed physician's visits and hospitalizations. When the company went public, 25 per cent of the stock was reserved for employee subscription."

Lena (Lane) Himmelstein Bryant Malsin occupies a strange place in women's history. She designed for women who were taught to be ashamed of something about their bodies, be it baby bump or buttocks. Her products were desperately needed, but not necessarily wanted.

Lena died in 1951, decades short of seeing any piece of social revolution that would urge women to love their "irrational" bodies. Many women still have a complicated relationship with her work today, both grateful and resigned. But that mentality is changing, and Lena is at the root of that change. She was the first clothier to tell women that there was more than one kind of pretty.

Her son put the power of his mother's legacy into blunt words in a 1975 article in the *New York Times*, written seventy years after Lena began to accommodate her nonconforming customers. Said Arthur Malsin: "The most notable change is that stout women don't feel like freaks anymore. . . . They wear sportswear, everything. They're not afraid to come out anymore."

Lena was the first successful fashion designer to understand that *no woman* deserves to feel like a freak. Her industry kept a century of woman feeling human while they waited for the rest of society to catch up with that truth.

WINIFRED SWEET
BLACK BONFILS

The news need not be so dry;
you'll sell more copies if you bring
a tear to your reader's eye.

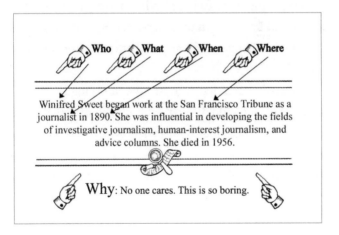

When a clickbait headline like "We Tested a Common Salad Topping for Rat Feces and You Won't Believe What Prince Harry Said About It Changing Everything in the Bedroom" interrupts your news feed, don't blame Winifred. She never meant for it to go that far.

All Winifred wanted to do was write news people would want to read. She colored the black-and-white columns of newspapers with the chaos of humanity, and journalism was never the same.

In 1874, Winifred was eleven, and she was orphaned. Her sister took care of her and allowed her to join a traveling acting troupe after she graduated high school. It was a way to channel a wild girl into a semi-controlled environment. It was also where Winifred started to study the psychology of how people take in information.

As an actor, Winifred hated it when the audiences laughed at the wrong time or got bored during poignant scenes. She became proficient at knowing these points: What do people want to hear? What makes them smile and laugh? What bores them or angers them?

And what happens if you put that into print, instead of on stage?

Eventually, she left the troupe and made her way through the still-Wild West to the offices of the *San Francisco Examiner*. The paper was owned by a spruce young upstart named William Randolph Hearst. (Spoiler alert: By the 1920s, Hearst would own the biggest publishing empire on the planet—largely because of employees like Winifred.)

Hearst was the father of what is called "yellow journalism." It's a judgy name to describe what was a new style of writing: telling a story with the rather tawdry aim of being *not boring*.

Winifred blatantly lied to Hearst about her abilities as a reporter. But that didn't matter because she had shown up at a fortuitous time. Nellie Bly had just blown journalism wide open by pretending to be crazy and having herself admitted for ten days to a madhouse. Newspapers were scrambling to imitate her actions, and an entire movement called "The Stunt Girl Reporter" was launched.

The *San Francisco Examiner* taught Winifred the basics of journalistic storytelling, and then told her to go make trouble.

Ever the actor, in January of 1890, Winifred squirted some belladonna in her eyes to make them overly dilated, put on her tattiest dress, tumbled from a streetcar, and threw herself into the softest pile of wooden crates she could find on a busy San Francisco street. The question she intended to answer: How would the people, police, and medical community treat a mute and distressed woman?

The people on the street were decent, trying to comfort her. Winifred worried that the whole article was about to go down the drain, owing to their kindness. Then the police came. Thus began a magnificent display of professional-grade rat bastardry.

Winifred acted dazed and sickly, not answering questions. The police took her for a drunken immigrant, dragged her down the street, and shoved her feet first into a black carriage. They took her to the San Francisco Receiving Hospital. Still acting dazed and unresponsive, she was put in a hard chair by the staff and a policeman, who glared at her for a bit and decided she was either drunk or poisoned. She reported: "One by one every person present stopped near me and sniffed my breath. The policeman was the last of all. 'No, I can't smell any whiskey,' said he. 'I wish to heaven I could say as much for you,' thought I."

That was the extent of her medical exam.

Luckily, in 1890s San Francisco, the cure for *both* poisoning and drunkenness was to force hot mustard juice down the patient's throat. Winifred disagreed with this diagnosis, silently but with a great flailing of limbs. One Dr. Harrison entered during this commotion and commenced to end his medical career. He declared that if she wouldn't take her medicine, the orderlies were to "give her a good thrashing."

Winifred again disagreed with the doctor's considered opinion and tried to scrabble away from him. He grabbed her head and pressed his thumbs into the soft tissue behind her ears until she screamed. He spun her by the shoulder and threw her on a bed. He took the skin off her shoulder in the process, and he told the medic to manacle her if she continued to protest.

Here, Winifred decided to end the experiment, and she gave the nurse a piece of paper with the name and address of a woman she'd prearranged to come get her when the question of San Francisco's medical preparedness had been answered. She then immediately wrote the entire experience up for the *Examiner* under her pen name, "Annie Laurie."

What happened next is evidence of the true power of the "yellow" journalism Winifred was providing. The public was engaged and enraged. This wasn't a dry fact sheet. This was a throbbing wound, a miscarriage of justice right in the reader's hometown.

To confirm her reporting, a male journalist returned to the hospital and confronted Dr. Harrison. The doctor affirmed he had manhandled his patient, but said she deserved it and that he'd do the same to any hysterical woman, based on medical principle. Then, judging that the noose was not nearly tight enough around his neck, the doctor followed the reporter down the stairs, telling just how many women in general would benefit from a sound medical beating.

It was, after all, only spoiled women who experienced public hysteria, which they did for attention. Amirite, bro? Bitches be crazy, right?

Bro?

Alas, this reporter was no bro at all. Harrison was fired.

Winifred's write-up was published Sunday. By Monday, letters had flooded the editor's desk. Specifically, they were letters written by rich women with prominent social positions. Winifred's writing had affected these women, and they, in turn, affected the powerful men in their lives.

The women of the city agreed that San Francisco needed kinder medical care, police intervention, and an ambulance service. Immediately. Thus, it was that even *without* the ability to vote, women's actions and voices had shamed an entirely male government to propose, define, and pass a motion to purchase two ambulances within a month of Winifred's publicized misadventure.

Example of the horse-drawn ambulance, with medical attendant, that Winifred helped procure

Winifred continued to write about social issues. Even when the "Stunt Girls" fad had faded, Winifred proved to have real writing chops. (Other, more photogenic Stunt Girl reporters retired and married millionaires fifty years their senior. I'm not naming names, but if I were to do so, one name would rhyme with *Smelly Thigh*.)

If anything important were to happen in the first decades of the twentieth century, Winifred was there, front and center, to report on the human element.

According to a *Time* magazine retrospective in 1935, when a storm surge flooded Galveston, Texas, in 1900, killing 8,000 people, "[Winifred] put on male clothes, shouldered a pickax, was the first reporter through the lines. Climbing over piles of corpses, she filed an exclusive story, organized an emergency hospital, got Publisher Hearst to send relief trains."

Signing of the Treaty of Versailles? Front-row seat, close enough to see the simmering resentment clouding the German delegates' eyes that would surely have no repercussions.

Lepers in Molokai? Too dangerous for most, but Winifred was the kind of journalist willing to risk a finger or two to humanize the suffering of others.

Whoremongering and opium dens off the Barbary Coast? Sounds like a fun weekend, but our wild woman reporter insisted it was business only.

Winifred sold papers. She brought a decidedly feminine touch to journalism. A news story that regales with drama and incites emotions is still news. She perfected the one authoritative feminine tone that early-twentieth-century men would listen to. Winifred became everyone's dearest mother—tender but firm, smart and reasonable.

Readers began to crave her particular voice to resonate through their Sunday editions. She began a column, syndicated throughout the country, simply called "Winifred Black Writes About...." Using her pseudonym, she also wrote a Dear Abby–style advice column, one of the first to be nationally syndicated.

Winifred continued to write until her death in 1936. Her style of writing never went away, but it did recede slightly, and was once again mostly relegated to the Women's Page.

Until a man discovered it afresh.

In 1973, Tom Wolfe wrote the groundbreaking book *The New Journalism*, in which he detailed the sort of writing that made journalistic nonfiction worth reading. He said the New Journalist used the following:

- Storytelling using scenes, not summary.
- Conversational dialogue instead of snippets or quotes.
- The narrator's point of view.
- Recording evocative details, friends, family, possessions, behavior.

Well, how original. Winifred Sweet Black Bonfils, now in her grave for forty years, turned over. Then she yawned, because Wolfe had described it all rather dryly, and besides, New Journalism was old news to her.

LILLIAN GILBRETH

We loved her so much for being "Mother,"
we sorta forgot about all the other.

Your kitchen is *on purpose*.

Whether that kitchen is a galley in a 300-square-foot apartment or is fitted with countertops carved of the same marble Michelangelo pulled his *David* from, there are remarkably few differences in the layout. Your sink is set into a countertop that runs flush to your fridge and stove. You have cabinets built directly under and above your food preparation area. And unless your architect was being a show-off, you seldom need to take more than three steps to move between the stove, sink, and fridge.

That didn't just happen. Even the nicest kitchens used to be tacked-on sheds or basement pits with random holes gouged in the walls for lead pipes to exchange pollutants in and out. Kitchens were disorganized and inconvenient, and using them actually hurt the women who spent most of their waking lives in them.

Even after the 1920s, after electricity and plumbing had been haphazardly installed in most homes, women still spent 50 percent of their time in kitchens. There, they performed a hellish Zumba of drudgery even worse than regular Zumba; it consisted of crouching, bending, scrubbing, reaching, stretching, and so much walking.

Then came this woman. Lillian is the reason your kitchen is so efficient that you never even notice it is efficient. She designed the now ubiquitous Kitchen Practical for the Brooklyn Borough Gas Company in 1929, and she scientifically reduced the number of steps needed to prepare a single dish from 281 to 45. That's about 6,000 miles of walking saved over a lifetime. Her design became the industry standard, and our kitchens today are still based on her layout.

But you don't know her for that achievement, nor for any of the other daily processes she streamlined and improved. You don't know her for her twenty-three honorary academic degrees or her very real Ph.D. You don't know that she was the first woman elected to the National Academy of Engineering, or that she was America's first female engineering professor.

You don't know that she's the only psychologist of either sex to have her face on an American stamp! (I'm sorry; now it seems like I'm yelling. My apologies. I just get really excited about Lillian. She's got her own stamp! Like Elvis!)

But the thing is, you probably *have* heard of her.

She's famous. Maybe the name rings a bell, or maybe your subconscious thinks she ought to look more like the actresses Myrna Loy, Bonnie Hunt, or Gabrielle Union. Because this pioneer of psychology and engineering is also the mom from the book *Cheaper by the Dozen*. She's one of the most innovative engineers of the twentieth century, but the world remembers her as "Mother."

ELEVEN PLUS HEAVEN

Lillian's "Dozen" was actually eleven, as her second child, Mary, died from diphtheria at age six. For the rest of their lives, and to the world they entertained with their story, the family still counted little Mary as part of their "Dozen."

She *was* "Mother," and she was good at it. She was also Dr. Gilbreth, and she and her husband Frank partnered to change forever how work was done in America.

Frank was a pretty cool, weird guy. He believed there was One Best Way to do everything. When he proposed to Lillian, he insisted they unite in passions both physical (she was pregnant thirteen times in nineteen years) *and* mental. He offered to quit his studies in the burgeoning science of energy management and take up comparative English literature and psychology, which were where Lillian's interests lay. Lillian chose to team up with him in engineering instead. They married in 1904, and together they pursued the One Best Way to Do Work.

Lillian was the only female in this field. She and Frank merged their talents to create Gilbreth Inc., and they became

SOME THINGS 1920S WOMEN HATED ABOUT 1920S MENSTRUAL PADS

(information collated by Dr. Lillian Gilbreth)

They Have Stupid Names. Johnson & Johnson's previous line of menstrual pads had been called "Listers." Bad, but better than their other frontrunner, "Flush Downs." "Modess" was appropriately vague and inoffensive for the era.

Asking for them by their stupid names. It was better if the store clerk was a lady, which they seldom were. Otherwise, you had to shamble up to the nice old grandpa chemist . . . or his pervy teenage stockboy and mumble for them to please go fetch for your vagina a month of blood catchers. Modess began to include discreet "silent request" coupons in their advertisements.

massively successful teaching businesses the One Best Way to do anything. Lillian focused on the humanity of a worker, particularly how being tired or unhappy affected performance. That was not something most business owners in the early twentieth century cared about.

Machines did most of the work by then, anyway. Unfortunately for the factory owners, humans still had to be around to press "on" buttons, and you couldn't thwack humans with a hammer if they were moving too slow. And they *always* moved too slow.

That's where Lillian came in. In a published study she did of a laundry in 1916 (Dr. Lillian Gilbreth was listed as a 50/50 partner on all but one publication with Dr. Frank Gilbreth, another first) she showed how a business could lose hundreds of dollars because of something as small as shoes.

Specifically, the shoes worn by the female workers.

In 1916, there were no comfortable work shoes for women *that also looked nice*. So, women wore pinchy shoes, got tired, and did poor work. Not something a man would ever think of, but this affected how much money got made. Plus, Lillian's psychological work showed you could not force American women to wear ugly shoes. (Frank encouraged women to wear European-style comfy clogs, but he was seventy years too early.) She found that if you compensated for those shoes with adequate rest breaks, however, production skyrocketed.

Besides success in work, the Gilbreths had a happy home. They ran their household as efficiently as a business, and it was as functional as any factory that employs three-

SOME THINGS 1920S WOMEN HATED ABOUT 1920S MENSTRUAL PADS

(continued)

The size of box they come in. Lillian found that the first thing nearly every woman did upon purchasing was to unpack the box and hide the pads. Modess began making boxes as small as possible, on a par with other common household items. Is it cornstarch, whale oil, or sanitary napkins? The important thing was that it was no one's business.

The color of the box. The brown paper 1920s stores wrapped parcels in wasn't thick enough to block color. If you bought 1920s Kotex, its loud, cheery blue screeched "Picture My Horrorshow Vagina" as you left the store. Which is totally cool in the 2020s, possibly even as a fantastic tattoo, but *tres gauche* in the 1920s. Modess began to make their boxes gray.

SOME THINGS 1920S WOMEN HATED ABOUT 1920S MENSTRUAL PADS

(continued some more)

The words and design on the box. The boxes were never repurposed. Questionnaire responses to that question yielded replies like "Hell, no!" And for the love of God, don't put "absorbent" or any other visual verbs on the box. Apparently "absorbent" was the 1920s cringe equivalent of "moist."

year-olds can be. But much happier.

In 1924, Frank phoned home to confirm he and Lillian's passports were all in order to sail to Europe for a lecture the following week. Frank hung up the phone and had a massive coronary, dying immediately. Or, as he would probably like to be remembered, with exceptional efficiency.

The depth of her mourning is unknowable; Lillian didn't grieve like other women. Now a widow with eleven children and no big savings to support her, she had some decisions to make. She boarded the boat to Europe two days after Frank's burial, alone, and gave that lecture.

What awaited her return would truly define her in women's history.

The majority of Gilbreth Inc.'s loyal clients waited a respectable amount of time following Frank's death, and then distanced themselves from the firm. She was blackballed from the industry she had created in the 1920s because clients had found themselves forced to deal with a woman.

Her children Frank Jr. and Ernestine later wrote, in their *Cheaper by the Dozen* sequel *Bells on Their Toes*, about their mother's revoked invitation to the world of men. And her determination to find her way back. "If the only way to enter a man's field was through the kitchen door, that's the way she'd enter."

So, Lillian embraced the feminine side of business. She consulted with Macy's department store for a few years, where she published one of the earliest scientific studies to

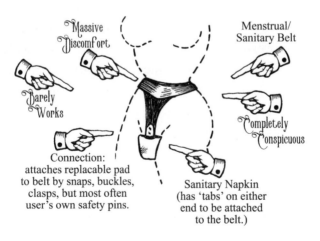

Basic Menstruation Gear Pre-Modern Age

Massive Discomfort

Menstrual/ Sanitary Belt

Barely Works

Completely Conspicuous

Connection: attaches replaceable pad to belt by snaps, buckles, clasps, but most often user's own safety pins.

Sanitary Napkin (has 'tabs' on either end to be attached to the belt.)

Pre-Lillian menstrual pads were so uncomfortable, they were almost a legitimate reason for women to be bad at math.

refute ageism. Hiring middle-aged women, discovered Lillian, was sound business. The average middle-aged woman was supporting herself and others, working double hard to compensate for the assumption people would have that she was old and tired.

Lillian began landing assignments with high-profile clients. She tackled women-centric issues that businesses had long avoided (but were worth a lot of commercial dollars). She did a groundbreaking study for Johnson & Johnson: a comprehensive market and consumer analysis of the sanitary napkin.

Johnson & Johnson had launched a sanitary napkin called Modess, with a calculated commercial potential of 45 billion products to be sold, but they weren't denting the market. They called in Lillian in 1927 to overhaul it.

She studied the box they came in. She also studied how the pad's shape, filling, length, and gauze weave, and investigated which scented creams women would rub on the cotton before wearing it. She found out everything there was to know about what women considered the perfect menstrual pad. Which is like conducting a study to determine which preferred brand of hobo you want to hug you while screaming dirty limericks on a streetcar; that is, none of the options is particularly desirable.

But Lillian did it, and Johnson & Johnson relaunched Modess as a top seller until it was phased out in the 1970s.

This is just a piece of the underappreciated work Dr. Lillian Gilbreth, industrial engineer and psychologist, achieved in her efficient life. That's why, though she was proud of the success her children had with their fictionized memoir *Cheaper by the Dozen*, she was troubled that her lifetime of achievements would forever be eclipsed by "Oh! You were Mother in *Cheaper by the Dozen*!"

She does deserve praise as a mother. She was a working mother who raised eleven children to functioning, well-adjusted adulthood. The pity is that history chose "Mother" to encompass her.

That definition is inefficient, vague, and poorly researched, which is the very antithesis of what Lillian stood for. So, we must remember the Lillian who also was a brilliant scientific pioneer who pursued human rights in the workplace, showing the logic that supported the shunning of sexism, ageism, and ableism. That's the One Best Way to remember Dr. Lillian Gilbreth.

4.

THE RIGHTEOUS SISTERS

GOODY-GOODIES FOR GOD

L o, and it came to pass, that at the turn of the twentieth century, God would speak to His people. He chose among the lowliest to bring forth His word: three unassuming women possessed of no great beauty or birthright. Through them He gave His urgent call: "You're all awful. I am going to burn most of you, particularly painfully if you drink beer. Please remain cheerful as I prepare your destruction. SING. I doth want to *hear* it."

At least, these were the messages relayed by *these* three women to an eager but baffled America. Meet three godly women who didn't just spread Christian values; they spackled them across the county with a trowel of righteousness. They were loved, they were hated, they were crazy, they were reasonable. All at the same time. We fondly call it faith. Amen.

ELLEN G. WHITE

The end is near,
but follow Ellen and you'll have (slightly) less to fear.

his is the story of Ellen G. White. She got hit in the head with a rock as a child, nearly died, and thereafter spoke to God in visions. Most women in history who make this claim are quickly labeled barking mad and suffer the consequences of their eccentricity.

The consequence of Ellen's claims was the foundation of one the largest Christian denominations on the planet. Ellen founded the Seventh-day Adventist Church, which today has 22 million members worldwide; owns and operates 8,000 schools, including thirteen fully accredited universities; and has an international healthcare system of 198 hospitals worldwide.

She's also the most translated female writer in history; her work (around 5,000 articles, forty books, and countless correspondence) appears in over 150 languages. Granted, there is evidence a considerable portion of her work was plagiarized. Which is a very ugly word.

Accurate, but ugly. Today's Adventist Church prefers the term "literary borrowing." An internal study in the 1980s indicated that about 31.4 percent of Ellen's work was "borrowed." The church gently reminds us that plagiarism was barely even a thing in the nineteenth century; authors copied each other all the time. Also, who's to say "God showed me that book and I copied it" isn't a legitimate form of divine vision?

Well, we might as well get all the eyebrow raisers out of the way, up front.

Some people (with medical degrees) have noted that her visions began directly after a severe blow to the front of her skull, and they have wondered about parallels between accounts of her subsequent divine trances and epileptic seizures. But that would be assuming God didn't guide that rock straight to her brain pan on purpose. Have you read the Old Testament? It's pretty intense. If God thought brain chunks were in the way of divine communication, He'd move them.

People also puzzle over her prophecies about the "Advent" in Seventh-day Adventism. The Second Coming of Christ at the End of the World. She had that pegged to happen within a few years' time of her earliest predictions in the 1850s.

Decades are technically years. And so are centuries. We haven't even racked up two full centuries since she first predicted The End.

Having been raised in this church, I can tell you that talking smack about Sister White will come to no good. You're asking to be sent back to your dorm room for the rest of day to sit under your cat posters with Bible quotes on them, all alone; and when someone finally brings you your lentil loaf, the gluten gravy will be cold. Also, you're that much closer to accepting the Mark of the Beast, being denied Heaven, and wandering in a Hell upon Earth for 10,000 years—and lemme tell you, that is a lot of stress to put on a fourteen-year-old! Like, she may be in her forties and still slightly shaky about it, for random example.

Let's focus on what Ellen did that can't be debated quite so hotly. How she managed, in a world where women were dismissible (religiously ranty ones, especially), to make her personal beliefs not just known, but embraced by millions.

First off, Ellen did not *rant*. How unseemly. Mostly she wrote, and though her manner wasn't particular fiery, her topics were. They struck a chord, a fearsome, perfectly timed operatic outro.

The mid-1800s were a scary time. Things were changing so fast. Uncontrolled industry, wars everywhere you looked, and wayward science were rebooting the world at breakneck speed. Maybe this was why a fervor struck Americans that the "End Is Near."

A Christian's most valued weapon against fear, especially of the world ending, is the Bible—specifically the Book of Revelation. So, it can be frustrating that Revelation reads like the fever dream of a madman. Angels pouring out cups, and whores of Babylon, and great serpents, and fire

A scene from Revelation, Chapter 8, where seven angels with
seven trumpets fill a censer at an altar and pour it on Earth, and
the world ends. Seriously, what's so hard to understand about that?

and death. You can tell it's urgent, that God needs you to know that something really heavy is going to go down . . . but what is it?

When Ellen raised a modest hand and said, "I know what it means. God has explained it me," an astonishing amount of people were ready to listen.

Thus evolved Ellen's specialty. Not so much predicting the future—she did a lot less of that as she grew older—but more fleshing out the confusing parts of the Bible and making its information accessible to the first generation of Americans who had enough time and schooling to not only read the Bible, but also be terrified by it.

Despite having a third-grade education, Ellen wrote (and borrowed) constantly. Her words were part common

END OF THE WORLD SPOILER ALERT!

According to Adventist theology, the End of the World will be directly caused by the Pope's influence. This is because the Pope is, or will be, the Antichrist. He is the Antichrist because it says so on his hat! Not his little everyday hat; a secret big hat, hidden in the Vatican. You see it in old paintings sometimes. It has numbers on it (disguised) that add up to 666.

sense, part steady old-time religion, and part hair-raising phantasmagoria. The formula proved intoxicating.

Ellen's husband, James, was good at distributing information. As early as 1849, he'd started mailing little tracts around the country to help comfort and unite Christians who believed Jesus's return was imminent. Taking advantage of the emerging "subscription magazine" fad, Ellen helped create an Adventist press in 1853. This began a mass communication never before utilized in religion. Her message was: "Yes, the world is ending, but here's the secret to surviving it"; that message circled the globe.

The money produced from the sale of her work distinguished her from other church founders, too. She tucked it back into the active parts of her religion. No fancy Tabernacles built; no personal wealth accumulated. Instead, she wanted schools and hospitals built in Adventism's name.

By the 1870s, it was possible for an Adventist child to go from cradle to doctorate without ever leaving an Adventist classroom. Affordable boarding schools helped ensconce children in the church's teaching, without worldly interference. Battle Creek College opened in 1874 with one hundred students, both male and female. In 1883, working under the quite insane but vivacious Dr. John Harvey Kellogg (the cereal guy, sorta; he invented cornflakes to quell animalistic urges, but it was his brother William who thought to add salt and sugar so they were sellable. And edible). Ellen saw the opening of Adventism's first nursing school at Kellogg's Battle Creek Sanitarium. In 1896,

Oakwood Industrial School, a training school for Black students, opened in Alabama. Soon Adventist educational opportunities spanned six continents.

Though her first schools were racially segregated, Ellen didn't particularly like that. Even in the 1840s, she was virulently antislavery, though many Christians (again, ugly but accurate) found it defendable by the Bible. After Emancipation, the Maine native had no particular problem with integrating her churches.

Everyone else did, though. When the infighting got too big, she told her people the most important thing was worshiping God, in *some* community, upon a sinful Earth, even if that meant segregation. It was far more important to get the worshiping done than to argue about color lines that would disappear any minute now, when Jesus returned.

Which was set to happen *annnny* minute now.

That attitude was one of many that struck early twentieth-century African Americans positively. Today, Adventism has the second-most Black American membership of any religion on earth.

As she arranged for medical missionaries to span the globe, and give medical and educational aid to poorer countries, Ellen's work at home focused on "preventive health" or Temperance. Many of her health guidelines are no-brainers today, but they were quite "spicy" in their time. Well, not literally. She thought spiced food caused immorality (and I dare you to prove it doesn't!).

Ellen said don't smoke and don't get drunk. Caffeine makes your heart race, so stop that nonsense. Don't eat meat; we haven't invented refrigerators yet (note: she didn't specifically prophesize refrigerators), so it will give you worms and makes you act nasty. And exercise! Sunshine is important. Stop masturbating, you degenerate monkey. Those parts of your body deserve honor and should be paired up with your heart and mind.

Sometimes people just came for the health stuff but stayed for the End-Times prophecies and complicated anti-Catholic conspiracy theories!

At the core of it, Ellen offered her followers the inside scoop on God's Plan. It's true, there were a lot of secret rules that only she could impart if you wanted to be sure of His favor. But all that secrecy and those special rules just made the religion more appealing. Nothing provides security like believing you alone have decoded God's ineffable mind.

Ellen died in 1915, before Jesus's return. The Seventh-day Adventist Church grew and grew, keeping her words (some faded when the prophecies didn't happen: England didn't join the Civil War to destroy America. At least not the Civil War *you're* thinking of! She might have meant the next one.) in the forefront of their mission, grabbing a foothold that stretched from Indiana to Israel by the twenty-first century.

Was Ellen a prophetess, guiding those who would heed her to the light of God? Or, was she a deluded plagiarist? I propose it's not binary. Ellen believed she was doing good; and then, she actually *did* some good. It's up to God to determine if she saved *souls*, but the hospitals, schools, and missionary services she set in motion can offer a solid tally of saved *lives*. As disappointed as she'd be to learn the world still exists, I hope she'd be pleased to see all the good caused by her prediction of its end.

AIMEE SEMPLE MCPHERSON

She surely meant well,
but oh what fantastic stories she chose to tell.

hen came Aimee. Most churches in the eighteenth and nineteenth centuries tended toward being glum and terrifying. Reminding fragile folks that they are but sinners in the hand of an angry God had always been the surest way to pack the house. But life brightened in the twentieth century. Many Christians wanted to see that brightness reflected in their church.

Onto this stage came a woman twirling in a diaphanous angel gown, rattling a tambourine, and leading catchy hymns of celebration: Aimee Semple McPherson. Founder of the Foursquare sect of Pentecostalism, she built the first megachurch, and was possibly the first world-famous evangelist.

What did she do? Well, different people will say different things. She might have done any or all of the following:

- Healed the sick by the laying on of hands
- Brought countless souls to salvation
- Faked her own kidnapping so she could abandon her children, have an affair with a married fella, pay a woman to act as her double, and lie under oath about the whole business

So . . . a lot! She did a lot!

Let's first look at the least controversial facts about Aimee. She was born in Canada in 1890, she married a Pentecostal missionary in 1908, and moved to Chicago. She gravitated to a life of adventure and went on to attain it in one of the few appropriate ways a woman could then. She and her husband went to China as missionaries, where he promptly got cholera and died. Aimee came back a single mother. She remarried, had another child, and tried to settle down, but the wanderlust and sense of larger purpose were too strong. She hit the road with her kids as a divorced, traveling lady preacher, which was quite bold.

Her career really took off at the Dreamland Boxing Arena in San Diego, in 1921. She crawled into the ring during a break in the match and announced she'd be there tomorrow, holding a week-long revival. The first night it wasn't well attended. So, to bring in more people, Aimee brought forth a crowd favorite: faith healing.

Faith healing is not as dramatic as you'd think. Aimee never explicitly claimed to have healed anyone herself—that's not how it works. She simply laid her hands, as biblically directed, upon the afflicted and prayed with them.

If their faith was sufficient, and it was God's will, their illness—whether it be a fondness for loose women or thyroid cancer—would leave them.

Did it work?

Well . . . sometimes it doesn't really matter. Sometimes connecting with a hurt soul accomplishes more than the most advanced medicine.

San Diego in 1921 was a very good place to practice faith healing. According to Pentecostal Theology's website, during this time "an estimated one in four newcomers to San Diego came for their health. . . . The suicide rate was highest in the country."

Whatever Aimee actually did for the faithful that week, whether it was a psychological frenzy or divine intervention, it was effective. By the end of Aimee's stay there, 30,000 people had surged the boxing arena, holding dying babies up toward her and shouldering tubercular parents, screaming for her intercession. She tried to speed up how many people she could lay hands on by climbing down from the ring, but she was so mobbed that Marines had to intervene and pull off her devoted followers.

Aimee quickly stepped away from faith healing after that.

But she'd made an impression. Shortly thereafter, she founded the Foursquare Church. She preached that joy, abundance, and even wealth could be integrated into a Christ-centered life.

Aimee was a crackerjack fundraiser. In 1923, she built America's first megachurch, the Angelus Temple, a palatial opera house of the holy that seated 5,000 people.

Angelus Temple

In 1924, from the third floor of the Temple, the first woman-owned Christian radio station began broadcasting (the second woman-owned station in history). It would broadcast for seventy-nine years. Aimee hired Kenneth Ormiston as her station's radio engineer. (Remember the name of that handsome young married gentlemen; it may be poignant later in Aimee's story. Or not! I might just have a filthy mind, subject to influence by muckrakers.)

Living so close to Hollywood, California, Aimee understood that the Christians of the 1920s did not respond to dour condemnations of biblical text, like their foremothers did. They wanted flair. Costume design. Biblical plays staged with Hollywood-level glamour. They needed some dang tambourine. (Aimee's favorite instrument, and probably also God's!) She provided all this and she became the most famous woman in America.

If we stuck to the bulk of information provided by Foursquare Church sources, the rest of Aimee's story would proceed thusly: Aimee helped the Foursquare Church feed the hungry during the Great Depression and successfully campaigned to remove pacifism from church doctrine during World War II while urging Americans to keep Hitler at bay. The End.

Again, that's not the whole truth. There's a *reel* of Hollywood-quality melodrama missing from that version.

One day in 1926, an incredibly popular yet still conservative Aimee went to the beach for a swim and some prayer with a friend. When the friend came back from making a phone call, Aimee was gone.

The search for America's beloved Sister Aimee was enormous. Divers scoured the ocean. A man died when he tried to swim out to a seal corpse that he thought was Aimee's floating body. She was feared dead and drowned.

Five weeks later, she stumbled across the Mexican border into Arizona, disheveled and thirsty but unharmed. She was subpoenaed to give testimony regarding a kidnapping. She said a car of people had begged her to come pray over a sick child. She'd been held hostage in a shack in Mexico while they sought ransom during the interceding weeks, until she finally escaped!

What an amazing story! The only problem with it was—honestly, every single word of it! Seriously, it was so bad.

Fifty separate people swore under oath that they'd seen Aimee staying at a cottage in Carmel with her married radio operator, Kenneth Ormiston, who'd disappeared during the same time. There was enough evidence to indict Aimee for perjury.

But Aimee was a consummate show-woman, and she had a one more reveal to prove her innocence. Okay, Kenneth might have been cavorting in Carmel with some trashy flapper while she prayed herself to freedom in a Mexican prison, but that trashy flapper wasn't her! It was Lorraine Wiseman! A look-alike, random woman who came forward to claim that it had, in fact, been *her*, not Aimee, who had broken the laws of God and Man in a sweet country bungalow.

Profile comparison of Aimee and Wiseman

That story might have held up—if Aimee had paid Wiseman more than $200 of the agreed-upon $5,000 for taking the fall.

Wiseman recanted the whole thing and told how Aimee had coached her on how to describe the bungalow's interior and its daily schedule, even told her the shade to dye her hair. Despite the holes in Aimee's story, all criminal charges against her were eventually dismissed.

Today, we pretty much take it as a given that celebrities who are held to unrealistic standards and who are hounded by fans and the press eventually have breakdowns. But Aimee was one of the first true celebrities in America. Her

Aimee jazzing it up for Jesus

radio station placed her in folks' living rooms, and she was an early example of the one-sided parasocial friendships (the belief that because we know everything about famous people, they sort of belong to us) that celebrities are better prepared for today. Aimee just wasn't prepared. It would have been overwhelming. She might have honestly thought she could just run away from it all.

After those events, Aimee was a media punchline, and her popularity plummeted. She responded by going "full flapper." She bobbed and bleached her hair, began wearing slinky gowns, and hung out with the glitterati of Hollywood. She built Aimee's Castle, a 5,000-square-foot Moorish palace of stone, turrets, and spirals, though church sources claim she sold it ten years later to feed the hungry.

Aimee stayed active but reduced her visibility in the church. The Great Depression had distracted the media and gave her a way toward redemption. But for most of America, Aimee was no longer the woman they needed her to be.

In 1944, Aimee was found dead in a hotel. The earliest reports claimed she died of heart disease, but a subsequent autopsy revealed her heart was fine—it just relaxed a bit too much after all the sedatives she'd taken that night. A lifelong insomniac, Aimee's death is generally believed to have been accidental.

Her obituary appeared in every newspaper, and each one mentioned the farce of her alleged kidnapping above all other aspects of her life. Is that a fair legacy? She pioneered a most peculiar corner of feminism—the kind of feminism that conservative Christians could embrace. The catch? To fully succeed, she had to let the people make her a saint.

She wasn't one, though. Sinless Sister Aimee was Aimee's *true* doppelganger, but just as it was with Miss Wiseman, she couldn't afford the price to keep her.

CARRIE NATION

Booze is sure to kill,
thus a few Hatchetations are surely God's will.

If God tells you to destroy illegal saloons by any means possible, planning is key. How shall one accomplish this sacred mission?

Appealing to the law wouldn't work; cops enjoyed a good beer as much as anyone else. Brute strength alone won't be effective, though even in middle age Carrie stood six feet tall and had a fair bit of strength. And arson is just plain unreliable.

Carrie had to find a different way to work God's will. Luckily, God told her He was absolutely okay with smashing, controlled burning, and hurling things.

This is what Carrie Nation is famous for. Standing at the threshold of an illegal saloon (most of the "joints" she attacked existed in dry states where alcohol was illegal), announcing something of inspiring grandiosity, such as "I am here to save you all from a drunkard's fate!" Or it might have been just a catchy "Good Morning, Sinners!" before smashing windows, mirrors, and bottles, and rolling beer kegs into the street to set them on fire.

She was arrested constantly, but that just made for fantastic photo opportunities. She was hated and abused, pelted with bad press, insults, and bricks. Prostitutes were hired to beat her up, since the male saloon owners (usually) couldn't bring themselves to punch a fifty-year-old woman in the face. Usually.

Yet she had an immense following; women who adored her shrill message declared they should have the right to vote, dress comfortably, and most important, not be subjected to the slow murder that alcohol perpetrated on mankind.

Carrie became a caricature, one she embraced. She sold souvenir pewter hatchets and pictures of herself looking every bit like the "veritable bulldog" of God she referred to herself as. She used the money, among other things, to post her multiple bails.

Carrie's notoriety usually ensured her a nice jail cell,
and she refused to be photographed without her Bible.

So, what makes a nice Kansas lady turn into a nice Kansas lady who chases fellas around saloons with a hatchet?

When a person believes they are doing God's work, they can be very difficult to reason with.

Born in 1846 Kansas, Carrie had parents who provided her little stability, moved often, and tried and failed at many different businesses, including running boarding houses. In 1867, Carrie married Charles Gloyd, a boarder in her parent's house. He courted her quickly but gently, tucking poems for her to find in the family's large copy of *Shakespeare's Complete Works*. He was a doctor, having been a field physician during the Civil War. She loved him. But he was more troubled than he appeared.

Civil War field surgeons were caregivers doomed to aid butchered men by butchering them further as they screamed for their mothers. The aftereffect of that trauma had no name in 1867, but it had a common treatment: booze, and lots of it. Charles Gloyd drank. Hard.

A year hadn't passed yet of their marriage before Carrie, now pregnant, was taken home by her parents. Gloyd was too drunk to see patients, and he couldn't support his wife. Nor could he speak to her or show her any kind of affection. He died of alcoholism six months after their daughter, Charlien, was born, in 1868. Carrie still loved him, and she was frankly blindsided by the breakneck pace of their courtship, marriage, baby, and his death.

Carrie married again, this time to David Nation. He was a man who was not a drunkard, but he spent little time with Carrie and, twenty-five years later, after Carrie had devoted all her affection and time to the Temperance movement, would divorce her on grounds of her deserting him. But he gave her the last name that would define her to herself. She legally changed her first name to match it, "Carry A. Nation." Onward! To sobriety and peace, should God will it.

And He did. He told her so.

He said, "Go to Kiowa." He *implied*, Carrie knew, "And take a sack of rocks for smashing."

Before we can marvel at the chaos Carrie created to get the results she wanted in a society that wasn't going to give them to her any other way, it's worth it to pause and ask, what in the world was this woman's problem? People drink! Always have. As for alcoholism, innumerable women have lost their husbands and marriages to alcohol. What was different for Carrie?

For one thing, her little tyke, Charlien.

Her only child, conceived in passion and fear with a sick drunkard. To know Carrie's life you must first hear about Charlien's.

Carrie wrote: "This my only child was peculiar. She was the result of a drunken father and a distracted mother. The curse of heredity is one of the most heart-breaking results of the saloon."

Carrie believed her daughter was born with mental deficiencies, though she wasn't clear about what they were. There was a prevailing school of thought in the nineteenth century regarding prenatal influences. (Here we are well to remember the majority of medical practices in the nineteenth century were based on thoughts, hunches, and a general mistrust of frequent bathing.)

"Prenatal influence" was the belief that a baby is heavily affected by its mother's emotional state when in utero. Mothers were advised to keep serene pictures on the walls of their bedrooms, remain cheerful, and keep a distance from ugly people. It went without saying that you should pick only a healthy person to be your child's other parent.

But when Carrie had a child with Charles Gloyd, she believed she had failed to practice any of those precautions. She knew, before the child was born, that her husband's alcoholism had stunted Charlien's life. In fact, alcohol had even more evil designs on Carrie's baby girl.

It was the ill constitution given to her by her drunken father, Carrie believed, that caused Charlien to develop an abscess inside her cheek as a small child. Soon, the skin rotted away, leaving Charlien's jaw exposed to the bone. A possible tetanus infection then resulted, with the child's jaw being clenched shut, unmoving, for eight years.

Carrie sent her Charlien around the country for medical help, often alone, since Carrie had to stay and run the motel the family depended on for food and shelter. Charlien endured suffering beyond reason; just as her father had performed the barbaric medicine of the era, Charlien was the recipient of it.

*Charlien in 1886, hands positioned
to cover the scarring of her wound*

Doctors sawed off a piece of Charlien's jawbone to create an artificial hinge, a surgery that failed. Skin was removed from her chin and used, in the most painfully primitive incarnation of plastic surgery, to cover the hole in her cheek. Her jaw was finally loosened in adolescence by the repeated and painful application of a prybar.

A prybar.

When our children suffer, we seek the cause. And we *despise it*.

In Carrie's mind, alcohol alone caused Charlien's suffering. Anyone who would support its sale and consumption might as well have been torturing her child.

Charlien was committed to a mental hospital in 1905, but she also married and had five children, and lived into the 1920s. We don't really know the degree or cause of her infirmity, but Carrie believed *she* did.

Which brings us back to Kiowa. In 1900, when she was fifty-five, Carrie took a train to that officially dry town full of not-so-secret saloons—or, as she called them "murder-mills."

She entered the (not remotely) secret back rooms, which women weren't supposed to do. That was okay; Carrie was gonna do a lot of things women weren't supposed to do.

The night she became Carrie Nation, the icon, was a raw and brutal joy for Carrie. She described taking her stash of rocks out of her bag: "I threw as hard and as fast as I could, smashing mirrors and bottles and glasses and it was astonishing how quickly this was done. The men seemed terrified, threw up their hands and backed up in the corner."

Riding high on this victory, she did the same in two other Kiowa "joints." Over the next ten years, she would be arrested thirty times for releasing her "Hatchetations" upon saloons.

Despite how many times she was arrested, Carrie didn't use *all* her photo and hatchet merch money for bail. One innovation she pioneered is often forgotten.

Most historical sources list the first American shelters for battered women being built in the 1960s. They overlook what Carrie had built: the first-ever Home for Drunkards'

Carrie and her merry band of Hatchetators.
Bring the kids! There's enough bricks for all!

Wives. Women and children moved into the furnished rooms, and the women were expected to get a job, but the shelter, food, and security were provided. The homes faded away in the interceding decades without Carrie to head them. The stigma that if you were foolish enough to marry a drunkard, you deserved what you got, needed an outrageous leader to refute it. Carrie's revolutionary belief that it was proper to be given safe housing in order to escape domestic abuse was the blueprint for women's shelters as we know them today.

If Charlien's suffering was the spark that fired Carrie's mission, her feelings toward men provided the tinder. Carrie did not trust the love of men. No matter how much she craved it.

"For years I never saw a loving husband that I did not envy the wife; it was the cry of my heart for love. I used to ask God why he denied me this. I can see now why it was. . . . Had I married a man I could have loved, God could never have used me. . . . The very thing I was denied caused me to have a desire to secure it for others."

Carrie died mid-speech in 1911, at age sixty-four. She was buried near her mother in Missouri, with the words she'd requested marking her grave, "She hath done what she could."

No man loved her save Jesus, whom she sought to serve by declaring war on the poison and its purveyors that made men into beasts, destroyed families, and crippled children. So, maybe it wasn't all about the booze, the spectacle, the anger. Maybe, for Carrie, it all came down to love.

5.

RUNNING HER MOUTH

**BIG-MOUTH BROADS,
CHANGING THE WORLD
ONE CRINGEY REVEAL AT A TIME**

he turn of the twentieth century saw an increase in women's voices agitating for social change—if the world wouldn't mind terribly the inconvenience, of course. After all, women's rights were very important, but it's never fashionable to be a Sassy Sue! You catch more flies with honey than with vinegar, you know!

Nonetheless, women began to use their words to gently suggest that maybe, at some point? If it was, in fact, convivial? In the future interested parties might consider skooching, a bit? On one or two small issues?

Thank you. I'm sorry. Thank you for your time. I'm sorry.

Upspeak and over-apologizing aside, there really *was* a place for gentlewomen with calm voices to sing a song of civility on many issues. Sojourner Truth, Susan B. Anthony, Harriet Beecher Stowe. All eloquent and important women who contributed to change using civil channels.

But some issues weren't civil. Some issues were brutish. Ugly. Violent.

In this chapter, we meet three women affected by loss and terror so deep that they needed to scream out a warning. And if that meant detailing your personal degradations at the hand of your husband, berating the nation's wealthiest men through a hail of gunfire, or openly humiliating half the country on the most private level possible, that is what they did.

This chapter might play a darker melody than its predecessors. Because a song will make you smile. But a scream will make you move.

ELIZABETH PACKARD

Husband has you committed on a whim?
Oh, the whole world's gonna hear about him.

F irst of all, Reverend Theophilus Packard should not have to *prove* to anyone that his wife Elizabeth is insane. Really, he shouldn't. Illinois Statute, Session Laws 15, ratified 1851. Page 96, Section 10:

> Married women . . . who are evidently insane or distracted, may be detained in the Hospital on the request of the husband . . . without the evidence of insanity required in other cases.

In fact, he didn't have any trouble for the first three years he had her incarcerated, starting in 1860, at the Illinois State Hospital. Her mail was intercepted, her six children were too young to help her, and even her parents thought she was as mentally ill as Theophilus insisted she was. He was her husband, after all.

But then the hospital released her, saying she was "incurable."

Her specific malady was "I don't want to be a Presbyterian anymore," and if the hospital had a treatment for that, they weren't able to make it stick.

So, poor Theophilus took custody of the madwoman God had burdened him with, and he did what any nineteenth-century husband would do in that situation: put her in a room, nailed the windows shut, and locked her in from the outside.

Now *that*, it turned out, was going too far. Legally, it was kidnapping.

Elizabeth managed to shove a letter through a crack in the window to the pump man on his rounds. She begged a friend for help. The friend went to one Judge Starr, and a trial was set to determine her sanity.

The trial commenced. Background was given thusly: Theophilus was a Calvinist Presbyterian minister. Mary was the daughter of a pastor, educated at a female seminary and very intelligent. One day she started suggesting the Calvinist doctrine may not be correct. Her husband brought two doctors who attended his church to examine her, barging into her room before she'd dressed for the day. She was terrified. They took her pulse, and she was committed to a mental asylum.

There are no scenes missing in that timeline. That's the whole thing.

However, during the trial those scenes were given more color. When the first physician to declare her insane, J. W. Brown, was asked to give the reasons he found her insane, he listed them (see box).

Kidnapping Mrs. Packard.

"Is there no man in this crowd to protect this woman!" See page 59.

No. 1.—"And this is the protection you promised my Mother! What is your gas worth to me!" See page 61.

No. 2.—"I will get my dear Mamma out of prison! My Mamma shan't be locked up in a prison!" See page 62.

A very disapproving but undeniably composed
Elizabeth being taking to the madhouse

PROOF THAT ELIZABETH WAS INSANE

(testimony of J. W, Brown)

- That she disliked to be called insane. [Hmm. That sounds like some verbally defiant dysregulated mood, right there.]

- An incoherency of thought. That she failed to illuminate me and fill me with light. [Do not blame the man for having high standards for the women in his community.]

- Her aversion to being called insane. [Make that "recurrent verbally defiant dysregulated mood," Missy!]

- Her belief that to call her insane and abuse her was blasphemy against the Holy Ghost. [There is biblical support that to abuse a child of God is blasphemous, but it obviously didn't mean girls.]

- Her belief that some calamity would befall her, owing to my being there, and her refusal to shake hands with me when I went away. [That was more likely just her ability to read the room.]

- Her viewing the subject of religion from the osteric standpoint of Christian exegetical analysis, and agglutinating the polsynthetical ectoblasts of homogeneous asceticism." [Well met, sir. If *Ghostbusters* has taught us anything, it's that any supernatural conflict can be halted with the use of ectoblasts. I think that's what he meant. Otherwise, what he said makes no sense at all.]

As Elizabeth recorded in her memoir about this examination, "The witness left the stand amid roars of laughter; and it required some moments to restore order in the court-room."

The second physician, Abijah Dole, put it bluntly: "She would not leave [the Presbyterian] church unless she was insane." The defense lawyer sought to establish the flexibility of Dr. Dole's religious tolerance.

When asked, Dr. Dole said that without doubt, the biblical tales of Jonah spending three days in a whale's stomach and surviving, as well as Elijah's ascending to Heaven in a chariot of fire (which contained wheels and seats and was drawn by live horses), were all literal events that bore no exaggeration. He concluded with an affirmation that Elizabeth Packard's belief she may worship God differently from himself proved her to be *completely* out of touch with reality.

The jury deliberated for seven minutes. Elizabeth Packard was found not insane. Her husband could not legally imprison her in her home or in an asylum.

Instead, just days before the trial concluded, Theophilus mortgaged the house (bought with Elizabeth's dowry money), sold all her belongings, took the children, and fled the state. Elizabeth had her freedom—and absolutely nothing else.

Elizabeth asked her legal team if she could recover her lost property.

"No," said my advisers, "you cannot replevy anything, for you are a married woman, and a married woman has no legal existence. . . . You are nothing and nobody in law. Your husband has a legal right to all your common property—you have not even a right to the hat on your head!"

"Why?" said I. "I have bought and paid for it with my own money."

"That is of no consequence—you can hold nothing, as you are nothing and nobody in law!"

Oddly enough, if Elizabeth had divorced Theophilus she would have regained a semblance of legal personhood. People asked her constantly, "Why don't you get a divorce?"

As satisfying as it would have been to see Elizabeth soundly slap Theophilus across his freakishly bearded face with divorce papers, she didn't want a divorce. She didn't believe in divorce. Nor did she deserve the loss of privilege that came with it. She said,

I have done nothing to deserve this exclusion from the rights and privileges of my own dear home . . . having done all the housework, sewing, nursing, and so forth, for my entire family for twenty-one years, with no hired help. . . . This self-sacrificing devotion to the best interests of my family and home, deserve and claim a right to be protected in it . . . instead of being divorced from it.

A divorced women in the nineteenth century would lose her home, children, community, her very identity. If there was anything a teeny bit crazy about Elizabeth at this point, it was her declaration that she'd happily return to living with Theophilus as his wife if he apologized and demonstrated what she called "practical repentance."

While waiting for *that* to never, ever happen, Elizabeth began a new mission in life. She now fought to convince the State of Illinois, and the nation, that married women were deserving of autonomous human rights. She wrote and spoke prolifically, telling how her family's messed-up dynamic led to her subhuman degradations.

Theophilius Packard in 1862 and 1872. Seems a man who embraces the hairstyle of a perpetually crowning fetus wouldn't be so quick to judge another's mental state.

The tale of her incarceration resonated throughout the country. Soon she was earning a living off of her story—enough to support her children. An 1869 article published in the *Chicago Evening Post*, entitled "The End of the Packard Matter," included a public exchange of letters between Elizabeth and her three remaining minor-age children, now all teenagers. They declared they were happy to come and live with her, provided they could still see their father and be allowed to follow their own religious beliefs. She agreed most warmly to these conditions, and the family, including the three grown children, were reunited.

Elizabeth made people think about having their freedoms taken away. Considering her ordeal took place during the Civil War, that topic should have been on people's minds anyway. But Elizabeth brought it out of distant Southern cotton fields and directly into the pretty parlors of Northern white folks. According to Dr. Samuel Wheeler, of the Illinois Supreme Court Historic Preservation Commission, Elizabeth "successfully lobbied politicians in Illinois to enact a new law, 'An Act for the Protection of Personal Liberty' that guaranteed everyone accused of insanity, including married women, a jury trial. Packard is credited with influencing thirty-four bills in various state legislatures, as well as success on the national stage, including an 1875 law allowing asylum inmates mail access."

Elizabeth's legal work even came into play when Abraham Lincoln's son, Robert, tried to have his mother, Mary Todd, committed in 1875. Elizabeth's activism afforded Mary Todd a legal trial (at which she was found to be quite insane, but determined so legally).

Elizabeth died in 1897, after having spent her last years living with one of her sons and his family. She and Theophilus never divorced, but neither did they ever see each other again. Theophilus had ruined his own reputation when he'd sought to ruin his wife. It might not have been the "practical repentance" Elizabeth had hoped for, but she likely accepted that result as divinely ordained justice.

MARY "MOTHER" JONES

Your business ethics are in doubt.
Mama's gonna knock you out.

Mary "Mother" Jones was *adorable*. She looked like a granny straight out of a fairy tale. Which is our first red flag: fairy-tale grannies are usually powerful sorceresses in disguise. In 1902, Mary had been deemed by one the many attorneys who prosecuted her for disorderly conduct not just cute as a button but also "the most dangerous woman in America."

According to the AFL-CIO profile of her, during Mother Jones's long career as a union organizer, "She was banished from more towns and was held incommunicado in more jails in more states than any other union leader of the time." In 1912, this sainted visage was charged in West Virginia with conspiracy to commit murder, for leading a march that turned violent. That was a capital crime, punishable by the death penalty. She was released only when public outrage pressured the governor to drop the charges.

Here's the puzzle. Mother Jones wasn't flashy; she dressed old and dowdy on purpose. She wasn't wealthy; she was an Irish immigrant who didn't have a permanent address for most of her life. She wasn't allowed to vote or hold public office; in fact, she didn't support the suffrage movement and she believed a woman's place was in the home.

So, how did she shut down million-dollar industries all over America with, according to one of many of her prosecuting attorneys, "a crook of her finger"? How did she make the Rockefellers and Roosevelts mind her? How did she help end child labor, twelve-hour workdays, and fatal disregard for the common worker?

Because it's impolite to argue with your mother, gentlemen. And you know you'll never win.

The real reason is that Mother Jones worked really, really hard to accomplish all that. She spent forty years in the pits with those who suffered. She referred to the men she drew into labor unions as "her boys," and she slept on their bare floors and ate at their meager tables wherever she went.

But many revolutionary women did the same, and they didn't end up infamous. What made her different?

What made Mother Jones different was her ability to use celebrity for her cause. She hacked away at civil injustice while "in character"—a tiny, sweet granny full of fire. She was an entertainer, an influencer, a paparazzi magnet. Which was really impressive, back when the paparazzi was just that one newspaper guy scribbling notes with a fountain pen while his buddy tried to balance a camera the size of your microwave on a tripod.

Mother Jones understood the media. She knew just how long the newfangled cameras required her to pause regally so that her face would end up on the front page. Her speaking voice was low and full, with Irish lace around the edges. It could fill an open field, with workers crowding around to hear her blunt and perfectly salty speeches.

Mother Jones was a soundbite delight, rattling off bumper-sticker slogans like "Mourn for the dead and fight like hell for the living!" long before the bumpers to hold them existed. At a fundraiser, when she was introduced as a humanitarian, she stepped up and shouted, "Let's get one thing straight! I'm no humanitarian. I'm a hellraiser!" Her speeches were simple and rousing, full of stories in which she did battle with a cruel oppressor and triumphed. And if li'l old Mother could do it, by God so could you!

An example of one of Mother Jones's "candid" shots, complete with angelic children, American flag, and the piercing gaze of righteousness

Though she worked mostly to unionize the male miners and railway workers, she knew it was their women and children who suffered when their men died, deep in the rock. She organized Broomstick Brigades of strikers' wives, armed with mops and broom handles, to beat off the scabs trying to cross the picket lines. She put women and children at the *front* of the protest marches, daring the strikebreakers to do them violence in front of reporters. Some would call that using a human shield, but Mother Jones and the workers' rights movement called it "a parade."

It was a blow to the burgeoning women's rights movements that she declined to lend her celebrity to their cause. To Mother, that was thinking small. She believed workers' rights encompassed women, Blacks, immigrants, children, and the disabled—anyone who wasn't getting, as she'd put it, "a square deal."

She also believed that any woman with the privilege of home and family should stay within it, fortifying it for those she loved. That wasn't a dismissal of women's value. The world Mother Jones lived in was cold, hard, and hungry. No, keeping a home fortified against all that might destroy it was a powerful profession. She should know. Mother Jones had no home address, but *Mary Harris Jones* had. That had been Mother Jones's name when her family had fled the Irish Potato Famine in 1847. She'd become a wife and mother in America, staying at home and tending to the needs of her husband and four small children.

That is, until 1867, when her entire family died in one vicious season of yellow fever.

A loss like that does not leave a person's psyche untouched. Still, Mary grieved by taking action, attending to other fever-stricken families in their quarantined homes. She was a skilled teacher and dressmaker, and she began to get back on her feet by opening a dress shop in Chicago. She wrote in her autobiography that she was uncomfortable with the difference between the women for whom she sewed ball-gowns and those who froze and starved outside her shop's window. The dichotomy was settled for her in 1871, when her business was destroyed in the Great Chicago Fire.

It was then, with nothing left to lose, that Mary Harris Jones began to become something bigger. She was helped to survive these tragedies by the labor union her husband had belonged to, and in turn began helping them. Perhaps in place of the family and career that had been taken from her, she adopted the downtrodden worker and his causes. Eventually, she became "Mother Jones" to the entire nation, the perfect figurehead for workers' rights. And she did not stop—not until her death (aged somewhere between ninety-three and a hundred and one, as Mother exaggerated her age) in 1930. Her work kept going, however. It reverberates every time a new workers' union is formed or a paternity leave is granted. The dimensions of what is a square deal change with each generation, but Mother Jones taught the world the calculus to continuously achieve it.

IDA B. WELLS

It started with a Memphis marbles game,
but she made sure the whole world knew their shame.

ost of the women I've had the pleasure to introduce you to in this book had experiences in which can be found a bit of levity. Ida's story is different.

Ida's story is one of evil. There is no levity here, and I won't try to add any. Her story is so astonishing that I want to tell it, but I want to make sure you know it's a rough ride before you undertake to read it.

Every feminist knows that Ida B. Wells was An Important Black Woman Journalist Who Fought Racism. She's become very popular in the past decades, and officially viewed as "inspiring." Heck, she's a Barbie now, part of Mattel's "Inspiring Women" collection.

Barbie-Ida comes with one accessory: a newspaper clasped in her perfect plastic hand. It's a good choice; that is the tool with which Ida changed the world. What's not commonly known is how offensive and deadly that accessory was, nearly killing the woman who was brave enough to wield it.

Born into slavery in 1862 Mississippi, Ida navigated racism her whole life, and she did not do it passively. As a young woman, she constantly caused white people trouble by insisting on being heard. She complained loudly and incessantly about the quality of materials available to the Black schools where she was schoolmistress. She was arrested (twice) when she attempted a Rosa Parks–type maneuver seventy years too early, by refusing to leave a (white) ladies' smoking car. She wrote endlessly in newspapers and spoke at conventions on all matters pertaining to the equality of women and Black people.

Despite living in an America reluctant to listen to her, she still believed in what we call the American Dream. In her youth, her ideals lined up with the more socially acceptable and ladylike Black women's-rights crusaders of the era: the members of the National Association for Colored Women. Their motto was: "Lifting as We Climb."

That meant, in part, a belief that the way to Black integration into a white-majority nation was to attempt to put the atrocities of the past behind and behave with consummate dignity and grace. To contribute to society through business, church, and community, and thus to show white America they had misconceptions about Black people and that those could be discarded.

Ida had believed in that—once. Then, in 1892, something happened that caused Ida to change. First her mind, and then the entire direction of racial equality in America.

A game of marbles. Just two boys, playing in the street, one Black boy, one white boy.

That street was in Memphis, where Ida was a nationally respected journalist for the Negro newspaper the *Free Speech*.

Two grocery stores faced each other on that street: one serving Black people, called the People's Grocery; and one for whites, called Barrett's Grocery. The Black grocery owner—Ida's friend Henry Thomas Moss Sr. (Ida was godmother to his daughter)—also believed in the American dream. He was achieving it, a respected man in his town with a thriving business.

The marbles game went sour, and the boys began to throw punches. Both Black and white men left their stores, perhaps intending to pull the boys apart. Instead, a deeper anger found an outlet, and soon the entire Memphis neighborhood seemed to be brawling in the street.

When six white men arrived the next night to ambush the People's Grocery in revenge for the fight, they were fired upon by the Black men who'd been anticipating the attack. Three whites were wounded in the exchange. Three Black men were arrested.

We tend to think of a *lynching* as a hanging, but the word is defined as any murder committed by a mob, without a government-sanctioned trial.

At 2:30 on the morning of March 9, 1892, seventy-five white men wearing masks entered the prison where the three Black men, including Ida's friend Henry Moss, were being held until trial. The white sheriff made no effort to protect the prisoners. They were taken to a nearby railyard and shot.

In the Hands of the Mob.

Henry Moss being led to his death, as depicted in an 1892 edition of the Memphis Appeal-Avalanche

Ida mourned. Ida was angry.

Ida was a nationally read journalist.

Ida published.

In her 1893 pamphlet "The Reason Why the Colored American Is Not in the World's Columbian Exposition," she included a chart she had compiled of Negro deaths by lynching, starting in 1882, with 52 Negroes murdered by mobs, and showing a steady upward trajectory year by year to 1891, with 169 Negroes murdered by mobs. These were, of course, just the murders on official record; she believed the actual number to be higher by hundreds.

Of the 800 murdered during this time period as listed on the chart, 269 were murdered based on a rape-related allegation, plus 5 more were for "miscegenation," or marrying a white woman. With the exception of those for murder, the sex-based lynchings amounted to more than all the other accused crimes put together.

Rape was a crime against honor and racial purity in the Old South, deplored even more than murder. A man accused of rape would have the fewest defenders, and the least amount of proof required to be deemed guilty.

Ida didn't think those numbers made sense. She asked her readers: Why do Black men suddenly rape white women, particularly when they know it's a death sentence? Why not during the Civil War, still fresh in living memory, when the chaos, rage, and lack of male defenders could have made Black-on-white rape commonplace? She wrote,

> The world affects to believe that white womanhood . . . [is] not safe in the neighborhood of the black man, who protected and cared for them during the four years of civil war. The husbands, fathers and brothers of those white women were away for four years, fighting to keep the Negro in slavery, yet not one case of assault has ever been reported!

Then, in bold transgression of traditional Southern delicacy, she backed up her theory with verification. She listed, by name and by town, Southern white women who had been in confirmed consensual romances with Black men. Women who'd given birth to Black babies but refused to name the father and would not accuse anyone of rape even to save their own reputation. She listed prominent women who'd fled north with their "colored" servants to live a domestic life. Black men saved from death by love letters, found in their pockets, from a white woman. Women who confessed at the last minute to infidelity, unable to bear the death of their illicit lover. With this information in order, Ida proposed her thesis.

In her pamphlet "Southern Horrors: Lynch Law in All Its Phases," she worded it bluntly: "White men lynch the offending Afro-American, not because he is a despoiler of virtue, but because he succumbs to the smiles of white women."

To be clear, that wasn't the first time she had set forth that absolutely unthinkable idea. The first declaration was in an 1892 article for the *Free Speech*, when the murder of her friend was still raw in her mind. She wrote the words that both marked her for death and shocked a revolution into existence:

> Nobody in this section of the country believes the old thread-bare lie that Negro men rape white women. If Southern white men are not careful, they will overreach themselves and public sentiment will have a reaction; a conclusion will then be reached which will be very damaging to the moral reputation of their women.

SOUTHERN HORRORS.

LYNCH LAW

IN ALL

ITS PHASES

Miss IDA B. WELLS.

Price. - - - Fifteen Cents.

THE NEW YORK AGE PRINT.
1892.

This is the literary equivalent of Ida's leaning across the table toward the most murderous racists in the South, speaking clear and low so she would be heard, and saying, "You know what? Evidence seems to indicate sometimes, white women just *like* sex with Black men."

The morning after this piece ran, a mob of white men showed up at the offices of the *Free Speech* to . . . well, likely slaughter everyone there. Which Ida and her publisher anticipated, so they were long gone, the building abandoned.

At first, the anti-Black newspapers thought the piece had been written by a man and called, in print, for his castration and death. Once safely in New York, Ida made sure everyone knew every bit of the combative, "filthy," and brutal language had come from her and only her. She was in exile. The *New York Times* labeled her "a slanderous and dirty-minded mulatress."

So, when an invitation came to tour Scotland and England, Ida promptly accepted. She was a popular speaker there, lecturing and publishing on the depravity white Southerners inflicted on their Black citizens. Unlike in the States, Britain listened. An 1893 issue of the *Manchester Guardian* got to the meat of Ida's effectiveness:

> Hitherto the outside world has heard only the version of affairs given by the whites, and although the own statements furnish abundant evidence for their condemnation, it is an advantage that the Afro-American's view of the situation should be presented. This Miss Wells does in a very effective fashion. Her quiet, refined manner, her intelligence

and earnestness, her avoidance of all oratorical tricks, and her dependence upon the simple eloquence of facts make her a powerful and convincing advocate. . . .

As tempting as it would be for Ida's Southern enemies to say, "Who cares what a bunch of pasty Brits think?" they could not. The British Isles imported the majority of the South's cotton, and Ida had been agitating for a boycott.

So impressed and distressed were the people of England that the London Anti-Lynching Committee was formed, led by prominent English politicians. They came to America to investigate if things really were as bad as Ida had described.

The people of the South found they cared quite a bit what Britain thought. Writes historian Paula Giddings in her book *Ida: A Sword Among Lions*: "If Ida had changed the discourse and attitudes about lynching, it was largely because the South had been exposed in a humiliating fashion before the cotton-importing exemplar of Anglo-Saxon civilization."

To refute Ida's claims, the politicians, newspapers, and businessmen had to admit, for the first time, that the South had a lynching problem. With the world now watching, they had to look like they were trying to stop the lynch mobs.

Recorded lynchings in America reached their peak in 1895, right after Ida sailed to Britain, and then they began to show a slow but definite decline. Though racism still broiled, the specific crime of mob lynching, according to the Tuskegee Institute, had no (recorded) occurrences by the end of the 1960s. Racially motivated killings still take place in America. They are now called hate crimes, ostensibly given special consideration with the convicting receiving harsher punishments. Ida's words—her refusal to speak politely—had begun the work that would eventually turn race-based murder from a casual secret to a nationally condemned outrage.

Ida fought against injustice, without ceasing, until her death in 1931. Her most effective tool was to keep saying things people didn't want to hear. She offended people; she annoyed and enraged them. Because she was willing to be loud, the balance shifted. Ida couldn't single-handedly stop racial hate, but she refused to allow the silence it needed to thrive.

6.

TOO FAR, TOO SOON

**SHRILL SHREWS
WHO DIDN'T KNOW WHEN TO STOP**

We all love a woman who'll go all out for the right cause.

We start loving her, oh, about a century after her death. When she's alive, a woman who thumbs her nose at the society the rest of us are trying to uphold can be really irritating.

The women in this chapter achieved tremendous things, supported by like-minded folks. Then they went a little too far. Their religion, their bluntness, even their *pants* made them too controversial for even their own supporters. As a result, they weren't given honorable placement in history's halls. Until now!

Hug your sister-wives and place your top hat at a jaunty angle, for we now have the pleasure of meeting three of the nineteenth century's most transgressive females.

MARTHA (MATTIE) HUGHES CANNON

How can you serve your country true,
if your religion makes everyone say "eew"?

In November of 1896, the intrepid innovator of the human-interest story (our own dear Winifred Black, writing as "Annie Laurie") traveled to Utah to meet a woman named Martha "Mattie" Hughes Cannon. A medical doctor and political activist, Mattie had just been elected the first female state senator in American history, twenty-four years before women had the national right to vote.

She won her senate seat by defeating her own husband, who was running against her. Her own husband, to whom she was not legally married. But he was definitely her husband. In fact, Angus Cannon was a lot of women's husband! Mattie was his fourth wife. Out of six.

Mattie was a first-wave feminist, an effective and groundbreaking senator, and a devoted Mormon, proud to participate in an illegal plural marriage.

This is the kind of woman we simply must meet.

Winifred got that. She came to interview Mattie as representative for an entire nation who were collectively cocking their heads and asking, "I'm sorry, what . . . what was that again?"

Mattie was willing to clarify all of it, and she gave Winifred a whizbang of an interview, leading with the reason women should be involved in politics.

> Women are better than men. Slaves are always better than their masters. A slave learns obedience and self-control and unselfishness. That's why women will do the world of politics good. They have been slaves so long. They will teach some of the slavish virtues.

Mattie was a blunt lady. Although, as far as the "slavery" of nineteenth-century sexism went, Mattie seemed less affected than most. Having emigrated to America from Wales as a small child to join the Church of Jesus Christ of Latter-day Saints (LDS), and watching both her baby sister and father die on the journey, she strove for self-reliance.

She demonstrated that virtue so strongly in her youth that she was chosen by the church elders in 1878 to be sent to University of Michigan to study medicine. She spent four years in Michigan and in Pennsylvania, receiving two medical degrees. The fact that a medical degree could be earned in two years might seem strange today, but not if you consider that there just wasn't much to teach back then. If you had mastered the application of mustard poultices and knew the best type of stick to give your patient to bite on while you were setting a broken bone, you were pretty much good to go.

Not to say it wasn't a rigorous regime. Mattie's UM medical class had 312 men and 40 women: only 77 men and 14 women graduated. Go Mattie!

In fact, "Go Mattie" would be the keynote of her life. First she went back to Salt Lake City, where she became the resident physician at Deseret Hospital. Back then, "resident physician" was a literal term. She lived at the small hospital and was always on call. That's where she met Angus, a church leader, who was twenty-three years her senior. The story goes they had a classic meet-cute when she told him to get out of her way while she was scrubbing a floor.

They married, by all accounts for love, in 1884. It was a very secret love, since even though many Mormons still believed in the holiness of polygamy, the U.S. government, which the area was trying to become a part of, thought that was gross. The Utah Territory officially abided by the 1882

Mmm. . . . Show me a woman alive who could say no to fine, fine whiskers like those.

Edmunds Act, which made polygamy illegal. Officially. Their first child, Elizabeth, was born in 1885.

But as for what Mattie thought about being a plural wife, she gave Winifred a pretty sweet sell:

> A plural wife is not half as much a slave as a single wife. If her husband has four wives she has three weeks of freedom every single month. . . . A plural wife has more time to herself and more independence every way than a single one.

That was her opinion ten years into her marriage and two flights from justice. It was a bit on the sour side.

In earlier days, there was much less slave talk and more declarations of undying connections of souls. She first fled the country with her newborn, in 1885, to save Angus from a polygamist's prison. Those letters were romantic, showing a young woman caught up in the excitement of sacrificing for love. Two years of bouncing around the UK with a sick child, reliant on near strangers, and keeping her real reason for "visiting" a secret (to many ears, *plural marriage* translated into "This hot desert flower needs some sweet tending to, sailor") shaded her outlook. She wrote:

> I have "stuck it out" so far, with the result of wearing myself out—so that I have no ambition left. . . . I am growing indifferent to everything that once gave me keenest pleasure . . . my poor precious baby feels the depression that is upon me . . . were it not for her and the religion of our god I should never want to see SL [Salt Lake City] again but seek some other spot and strive to forget what a failure my life has been.

She would return home eventually, where waited the less romantic business of sustaining any marriage, especially a complicated and illegal one. She would never share a roof with her husband. He took two more wives. They fought a lot. It was rough.

So, Mattie built a little house of her own and continued her medical practice. She saw her husband rarely—enough to conceive their second child, James, in 1890. (This caused another, briefer, and more enjoyable exile to California, once again to protect her husband from polygamy charges.) Meanwhile, she grew into a bit of a political powerhouse.

Mattie helped make sure that women's suffrage was written into the state constitution when the territory was accepted into the Union in 1896. Because she was an educated lady and was married to a church leader, she found herself on many committees, giving hundreds of speeches. Eventually, she was nominated by the Democratic Party to run for one of the seats in the newly formed Utah State Senate. Strangely, she wasn't the only Cannon nominated to run. Or, as she put it to Winifred:

> They [the Democratic Party] thought there ought to be a lady in the Senate, and a committee came and asked me if I would run and I said yes. . . . Then I went home and congratulated Mr. Cannon on his [Republican] nomination.

Of the five seats from Salt Lake County available, Mattie won one of them. Angus did not. One contemporary newspaper summed up the contradiction of Mattie's election succinctly: "Mrs. Cannon believes in polygamy, and is a victim of it, if victim she can be called when she can whip her lord and master at the polls."

1897 Utah State Senate. Mattie on the left; the other two ladies are secretaries—which was also mostly a man's job at the time. When you think progressive, start thinking nineteenth-century Utah.

She was good at her job, too. While in office, only one bill proposed by Mattie wasn't passed, one to teach school-children the dangers of narcotics and alcohol. Her other undertakings—procuring education for "deaf, dumb, and blind" children, creating a State Board of Health, and forcing employers to allow female employees to sit down during the day—were slam dunks, sensible and supportable. She served two terms, and there were rumors of sending her to the U.S. Senate.

Then she had a baby. Little Gwendolyn, her third child, was born in 1900, and she was loved. But she was also evidence.

Angus proudly acknowledged this "illegal" baby was

Mattie with Baby Gwendolyn,
or as federal prosecutors might refer to her, "Exhibit A"

his and his fourth wife's. He said while the Mormon church might have agreed with the U.S. government to make it unlawful to take *new* plural wives, he would never abandon the ones he already had. He was arrested, but got off lightly with a $100 fine.

Mattie was never in danger of being imprisoned, but her political career was over. Simply put, it was against the law to be a polygamist. She couldn't represent herself as a lawmaker while openly defying the law.

She ended her term in the state senate and spent the next fifteen years moving between Salt Lake City and California, where she would eventually settle, far from Angus.

Until his death in 1915, at age eighty-one, their correspondence grew increasingly angry and resentful. Maybe she blamed him for her losses. She never openly participated in politics again, nor did she ever again officially practice medicine. That frustrated Angus desperately. He was already living off his "brethren's charity" to support his six wives and twenty-six children. He told her it would be nice if she'd stop asking him for an allowance and make her own money.

As for why she didn't practice medicine after working so hard to become a doctor, historians point out that Mattie's medical degree was awarded to her *right before* medical knowledge exploded. X-rays, vaccines, germ theory, even aspirin—all became common immediately *after* she had learned how to be a doctor. It is believed Mattie did not trust herself to practice well. That might have been for the best, since we know she was regularly dosing herself with sea air and strychnine to treat her own heart problems.

Mattie had made prescient remarks when talking to Winifred, saying things like, "Electricity will soon do away with much of the domestic drudgery. Women are growing wise and men are growing gentle. I think the millennium is coming sooner than we dare to hope."

It didn't come soon enough for Mattie. Her remaining years were many (she died in 1933), but not very happy.

Mattie was a feminist of nearly modern caliber, balancing a complicated personal life with a demanding career. She moved obstacles to improve the world while privately having opinions and practices that repulsed society. Her downfall came as a result of hoping society would grant her religious tolerance—accepting that she worshipped the same God most nineteenth-century Americans did, but in her own way and without secrecy or shame. Mattie was living proof that a person could hold contrary beliefs and still add value to the world. Someday, that lesson might take.

MARY EDWARDS WALKER

You might be a war hero before your time;
doesn't matter if . . . PANTS! PANNNTS!!!

Mary was raised to believe she was equal to men. Since she was raised in the early nineteenth century, this belief was way, *way* off. But she never abandoned it. And the entire country tried to get her to do so.

Mary was born in 1832, in Oswego, New York, to parents so hard-core anti-establishment they would have been forcibly removed from Burning Man for undignified behavior. They eschewed all traditions and gender roles, starting the first free school in the state, which was, of course, co-ed. Her father was a self-taught country doctor. Which, granted, sounds terrifying; but then again it was still the days of leeches treating pneumonia and bad humors causing dropsy, so "terrifying" was expected from the medical profession. Young Mary's house was full of medical texts, which made her want to be a doctor. She went to Syracuse Medical College when she was twenty-one. Which . . . wasn't . . .

the most respectable medical school. Some would argue it wasn't really a medical school. But it still graduated people called doctors, and Mary was the single female among those graduates in 1855.

Mary wore pants. Even though we all know a woman is at her most appealing when she cannot walk, bend, or breathe with ease, Mary insisted her clothes be practical. Even before Amelia Bloomer gave her name to what was generally considered a failed attempt at dress reform, and long after the fad had run its course, Mary wore pants.

Both during her lifetime and long after, people had decided "wearing pants" was the most important thing about her. It really wasn't.

The *Brooklyn Daily Eagle* described her "costume" in 1866: "Without the least suspicion of vulgarity or indecency, it is nevertheless not a kind of dress which the women of either England or the U.S. will ever adopt." The reporter was quite right. Just as Lillian Gilbreth (see page 93) taught us most American women would *not* wear ugly shoes, Mary taught us that their disdain for goofy-looking skort sets was even stronger. Goofy suited *her* quite well, though. Her most memorable response to the continued question, "Why do you wear men's clothes?" was the response, "I don't. I wear *my* clothes."

That same article briefly touches on the fact that, above the pants, Mary also wore the Congressional Medal of Honor—the only woman ever to be awarded one. What was that compared to pants, though?

She wore pants to her wedding, in 1855, to a fellow Syracuse medical student. She also kept her maiden name, removed the word *obey* from the marriage vows, and worked side by side with her husband in a joint medical practice. Which was unsuccessful—both the medical practice and the marriage. Mary threw her husband out after four years when he cheated on her. This was no small feat, though; 1850s New York didn't like divorce and made applicants wait five years before granting one.

Alone, she started a medical practice so "those who prefer the skill of a female physician to that of a male have now an excellent opportunity to make their choice." Which was terrifically optimistic of her. The practice folded immediately, from lack of patients. Luckily (at least in the sort of life Mary lived), that was when the Civil War broke out.

Mary showed up at the area's Union Army recruiting office, offering her skills as a surgeon. They said no. There'd never been a female surgeon in the army. There'd never been a female in the army. They offered that she could be a civilian nurse, but Mary refused. Nonetheless, she was present and helping where she could during the entire war. Since the army wouldn't hire her, she served as an unpaid volunteer, treating soldiers and civilians in a field hospital.

How good a wartime doctor Mary was we'll never know; there are no objective sources. Anyone with medical knowledge and a strong stomach was valuable during the war. But that same medical knowledge, if attached to a vagina (especially one in trousers), was certainly not appreciated during peacetime. After the war, many people said she'd been a poor doctor, but they honestly might just have been being jerks. I mean, people *really* hated her pants. Dr. Roberts Bartholow, who served with Mary in the Army of the Cumberland, recounted in an 1867 edition of *New York Medical Journal*, "She had never been, so far as we could learn, within the walls of a medical college or hospital for the purpose of obtaining a medical education."

Eventually, the U.S. Army employed her as a Contract Acting Assistant Surgeon (civilian). And thus, Mary was the first woman to be "hired" by the American military.

Mary worked through the Battle of Bull Run and the Battle of Fredericksburg, among many others. She didn't like the Civil War cure-all: limb amputation. She fought against using it; she thought proper hygiene and time could heal a wound, and she demanded the soldiers be told their chances of recovery before agreeing to lose their arms and legs. This didn't add to her popularity.

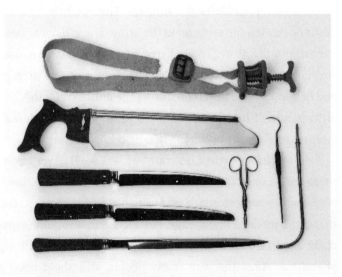

A Civil War surgeon's tools for amputations.
(*Source: National Archives*)

Since Mary worked very close to the front lines, she often cared for civilians living in Confederate-held territory. She crossed the enemy lines so frequently and so casually that she wrote to the State Department and asked if they would like her to spy. She had such impunity in the Confederate camps that it really would have been no extra effort. Literally, just stand a little closer to the general's tent, maybe ask his aides where they were heading tomorrow; should she wear her mountainous-region ambush pants or, say, open-frontal attack pants? But the Union Army said no. Not that it mattered; in 1864, she was arrested as a spy anyway, and spent four months in a prison camp, before being released in a prisoner exchange.

After the war, Mary threw herself into the social hot-button issues of the time: healthy living, clothing reform, and women's rights.

She spoke often, and people say she was quite terrible at it. An 1866 article describing her speaking tour in London wasn't exactly chuffed with her oration: "after she had proceeded with her strange combinations of pathos and pantalettes, physiology, clinical operations and negro emancipation, with no apparent purpose of striking into a line of connected narrative or argument."

Most of the news regarding the rest of Mary's life continued in this vein, mocking and resentful. So, you saved some lives and risked your own to comfort and cure under enemy fire? You think that gives you basic human rights and agency over your own body? Not in *those* pants, honey.

Mary and Carrie Nation (see page 127) lead a proposed
"Chamber of Female Horrors," full of irritating women.
(Source: 1901 Puck cartoon)

Even if her speeches wandered a bit, her heart was deeply aligned with women's rights. Well, *aligned* is the wrong word. She diverged from most suffragists in a big way—so much so that they stopped asking her to hang out with them. Mary believed that the Fifteenth Amendment *already* granted her, as a citizen, the right to vote, since it granted *all* citizens that right. No further amendment was needed. When the more successful suffragists started pushing for a separate amendment to allow lady voters, Mary parted ways with them. As often happened for the women we've met in these pages, even their own "tribes" disliked how they agitated.

By the late 1800s, Mary had gone full fancy fella. No more awkward bloomer-and-skirt sets. She went about town in a dinner-jacket ensemble, complete with top hat and gentleman's walking stick. Which was illegal, and Mary was arrested often for cross-dressing. Elizabeth Cady Stanton and the other leaders of the suffrage movement believed Mary's wearing garments with crotch-suggesting inseams (pants!) would not win over the doubters that women could be fully female, dignified, and decisive. To defy society so brazenly, even with a Medal of Honor on your waistcoat, was a tetch of tone deafness that they

didn't think helped the greater cause of women's rights.

About that medal. When the Civil War ended, Mary wrote to President Andrew Johnson and asked for written proof she'd been a commissioned officer (her medical rank would have been akin to that of Major), so that she would receive her pension. He didn't want to commission her. So, he sent her a Congressional Medal of Honor instead, to shush her.

Today, there is no higher military accolade than the Congressional Medal of Honor, and it is awarded for extreme valor under fire. But in the mid-1800s, the Medal of Honor was the *only* medal that the government gave, and they handed them out like a dentist hands out tiny toothpastes. There are records of men being given the Medal of Honor for delivering a letter across town, for stamping out a camp-fire, one was even given to a guy who wrote and asked for a souvenir.

What changed? Well, in 1916, in the midst of World War I, the U.S. Army said, "We really should have more rules for giving these out." Under directions from Congress, they reviewed the past recipients; 2,624 men plus Mary, and then took away 910 of the medals from once-honored, now old and certainly devastated men.

And one Mary.

The biggest reason to lose your medal was not having been an actual soldier commissioned by the army. Mary had been—not for lack of trying—a civilian. So, Congress decreed that if a person's medal was recalled, "the name of the recipient of the medal so issued shall be stricken permanently from the official Medal of Honor list. It shall be a misdemeanor for him to wear or publicly display such medal. . . . He shall be required to return said medal to the War Department for cancellation."

Now, you'll notice that, technically, they said, "he." That looks like a raging loophole to me! And perhaps to Mary, too, for when Mary got the notification to return her medal, at age eighty-one, it is said her reply was, "Let them come get it." She believed she had earned that medal, and she wore it every day for the rest of her life. Afterwards, too, because she was buried with it on her chest.

In February of 1919, Mary took a fall on the Capitol steps and died soon after. In June of that year, Congress passed the Nineteenth Amendment to the Constitution, allowing women to vote. Mary didn't live to see it, nor to see the official reinstatement of her Medal of Honor in 1977. Not that she would have cared. She knew her value and her rights, even if it took the rest of the country a century to catch up.

BRADY, PHOTO, NEW YORK.

VICTORIA WOODHULL

She wanted marriage reform to make women safe,
but too much free thought made society chafe.

Victoria is famous because she was the first woman to run for president of the United States, almost fifty years before women were allowed to vote. But she didn't really want to be president; and even if she did, it's one of the least interesting things about her.

She was born Victoria Claflin, her father a one-eyed con man and her mother a mentally unstable religious fanatic. When she was a child, her dad was run out of town for a dreadfully artless attempt at arson. Then to rid themselves of the entire Claflin scourge, the local church held a fund-raiser to make sure his wife and passel of children were shipped out after him.

So, where does a girl go from that inglorious beginning? Oh, but she does go far!

Post-banishment, Mr. Claflin chose his two most astute daughters, Victoria, age fourteen, and her little sister

Tennessee, age seven, as primary breadwinners for the family, and he presented them as clairvoyants. They did very well. They were smart girls, with a gift for comforting the endless barrage of adults who came to them in pain and desperation.

Twenty-eight-year-old Dr. Canning Woodhull was called to treat fourteen-year-old Victoria for fever. By now we understand that "doctor" in this era did not always represent a specific skill set or education level: certainly, it was thus in Canning Woodhull's case.

He was called "Doctor" by the same principles for which you'd name your cat "Professor Swishybutt." Not really qualified for the title, but don't tell *him* that. Woodhull married Victoria right after her fifteenth birthday.

He was an abusive drunk, and by age sixteen, Victoria had a son, Byron, who had severe mental disabilities. She was obliged by law to remain with Canning Woodhull for the rest of her life.

These were the seeds of Victoria's purpose. Bad marriage destroyed the lives of young nineteenth-century girls. Truth was, she wasn't all that interested in voting reform. She got involved in voting rights because suffrage was the only credible platform for women to speak on the world stage. But what did politics matter when a woman's home life was a prison?

Victoria didn't go shrieking her revolutionary ideas about marriage into the public ear, at least not right away. Instead, she and her sister found a much more respectable door into fame and influence. As successful clairvoyants, they found themselves an ally in the uber-wealthy Cornelius Vanderbilt. Vanderbilt is often mischaracterized as the richest man in American history. He is not. He is the second richest. (Curse you, Rockefeller.)

Vanderbilt was, surprisingly, a Spiritualist himself. Less surprisingly, he quickly fell in love with twentysomething Tennessee, whom he cuddled on his eighty-year-old lap and called his "little sparrow."

Here formed a partnership that gave Victoria remarkable clout. She would go into trance and give Vanderbilt tips from the finest ghosts of finance, and he'd give her tips based on having billionaire-level financial experience. The end result was Victoria and Tennessee's forming the first-ever woman-owned brokerage firm. They made $700,000 (in 1860s dollars) in six weeks during the market crash of 1869, cementing their reputation as respectable brokers. All this while bearing the unfortunate deformity of their private parts not being the dangly kind.

Victoria's money and popularity allowed her to start her real passion: a newspaper, called *Woodhull & Claflin's Weekly*. She pledged against mudslinging, a promise she would not remotely keep, and she gained a circulation of 20,000 subscribers by the end of her first year. It was here that she was able to preach her message of marital equity. Which is what she should have called it! Instead, she called it "free love."

Caricature of Victoria by Thomas Nast:
"Get thee behind me, [Mrs.] Satan!" Wife, with
heavy burden, states: "I'd rather travel the hardest
path of matrimony than follow your footsteps."

"Free love" called to mind a giant orgy pit of smelly, sweaty, fleshy vice. That wasn't what she meant. She believed a woman being trapped in a bad marriage was the root of nearly all unhappiness. Still, she declared her position loudly and without apology:

To those who denounce me I reply: "Yes, I am a Free Lover. I have an *inalienable*, constitutional, and *natural* right to love whom I may, to love *as long* or as *short* a period as I can; to *change* that love *every day* if I please, and with *that* right neither *you* nor *any law* you can frame have *any* right to interfere."

All she wanted was full social and sexual equality for women, precluding them from any judgment that wouldn't be levied on a man in equal measure. She wanted this immediately, in 1872.

It was not available.

Nor was it available in 1972.

But we all have high hopes regarding 2072.

Victoria showed the double standard for promiscuous men versus women by revealing the secret life of the most popular preacher in America, Henry Beecher. In her eyes, he was . . . well, there isn't really a masculine version of "two-faced slutbag." I would humbly propose, after researching the good reverend thoroughly, we could start using *his* name *as* that slang. You'd know the kind of man I was referring to if I called him a "total raging Beecher." It was an open secret he had nonstop affairs with innumerable women.

Victoria was a friend of the Beecher family, and she, too, kept that secret for him. For a time. Technically, Henry Beecher was practicing what she herself preached: loving whom you wanted, when you wanted, without social or government interference. The problem was, he was not practicing what *he* preached. She said he knew this, and he begged her not to tell the world what an utter Beecher he was. "He got up on the sofa on his knees beside me, and taking my face between his hands while the tears streamed down his cheeks, begged me to let him off. Becoming thoroughly disgusted with what seemed to me his pusillanimity, I left the room under the control of a feeling of contempt for the man."

His sisters, Catharine and Harriet (yep, Harriet "famous author who wrote the novel people say started the Civil War" Beecher Stowe), openly wished death upon Victoria. Catharine accepted an invitation for a carriage ride with Victoria to discuss their differences and find peace. They did not succeed! According to Victoria, the ride ended with Catharine Beecher's parting words: "Remember, Victoria Woodhull, that I shall strike you dead."

As for Harriet, well, if you start a nineteenth-century morality war with the person who wrote *Uncle Tom's Cabin*, you're not going to win. Harriet detested Victoria. She wrote a book called *My Husband and I*, which featured a progressive feminist villain with the achingly subtle name of Audacia Dangyereyes, based on Victoria. Harriet trashed her in church-owned media.

THAT BEECHER CREATURE

Henry Beecher (pictured here with one of the few women he never tried to sleep with, his sister Harriet) eventually went on to have his own trial for adultery. The particular mistress whose husband accused him had written her confession years prior. Then recanted. Then reissued. At any rate, he was cleared of all charges and retained his stature as America's favorite Christian leader, despite being a shameless, disgusting Beecher. It's just different for men, sometimes.

Victoria clapped back in her own paper. She defended herself well, but she was a mega-liberal, loud "free love" advocate trying to bring down two of America's treasures.

At that point, Victoria was done playing nice. She wrote in her newspaper in excruciating detail of Beecher's affair with his colleague's wife, also mentioning the disgusting behavior of a venerable Wall Street trader who held up bloody fingers at a party as a token of a young girl's virginity he'd just claimed.

It was customary for leaders of the suffrage movement to queue up to cast their illegal ballots on Election Day. Victoria, on the ticket of the Equal Rights Party for president, was scheduled to do this in 1872, but could not attend because she was sitting in prison on charges of indecency—for using the words *token* and *virginity* in print.

Victoria was very slowly cleared of all charges, though she was arrested a few more times for good measure. Her eccentricity was used against her. Her first husband still lived under the same roof as she and her second husband (the terrifically named Colonel Blood). She was penniless because of mismanaging her earlier fortune. Her family was sketchy. She was mentally unstable, claiming to channel dead Greek philosophers. Every bit of this was true, of course, but there was no need to be so nasty about it.

Exhausted and disheartened after screaming for justice in a world not the slightest bit interested in hearing about it, Victoria changed. Her paper stopped lauding Spiritualism and began to run articles on how the Catholics actually had a pretty good system. By the time she was middle-aged, she began avowing she'd never actually been a proponent of free love but, rather, was a puppet of the men who surrounded her. She shuttered her brokerage, her newspaper, and her life as an agitator.

Victoria spent the later years of her life tucked away in an English village. She found love with her third husband, a wealthy banker ten years her junior. She died at age eighty-eight, in 1927, in England.

Victoria wasn't in the women's suffrage history books because she was actually rather "meh" on political suffrage. She wasn't in the political history books because her contributions in that area were something even she didn't take seriously. But her core message, "treat women fairly," was historic; it was just too simple and reasonable for a society as complicated as ours to understand.

CONCLUSION

BE DREADFUL

*S*tatistically speaking, you're probably not a prophet of God, a billionaire financier, a single mother of twelve, or a whistle-blowing journalist who now needs to flee the country.

But you have *a lot* in common with the women you've met here. Like these women, there are things you desire. Things that the world isn't going to help you get.

Sure, you can legally wear pants now. Men probably aren't after your reindeer, nor do they restrict your scientific research to maxi-pad tests in a home laboratory. We're proud to have grown.

But we've been careful not to grow *too* much. There are still rules for being a true and proper woman. There are still limited options if you want to fit smoothly, to not draw attention to yourself and to not irritate people.

And there are still punishments.

If you try to be too different, you'll lose credibility, acquaintances, and invitations. When you're slammed for being an attention whore, a bad mother, a selfish bitch, a skank, a liberal whack job, or a brainwashed housewife, you're feeling what these historic women felt.

Unsuitable. Unbecoming. Not enough. Same sentiments, just new names.

So, following our role models, here's what you do if you're truly unbecoming as a lady. If, like the women you've met here, you find you can't squeeze into the space society has slotted for you, sit quietly and contemplate the dimensions of the area they're asking you to fit tidily into. Get to know it's boundaries and its restrictions. Here are some examples you might feel familiar with:

I CAN SHARE MY LIFE ON SOCIAL MEDIA . . . but just the cheery parts and not too often. No need to make a spectacle!

I CAN PURSUE MY CAREER . . . but not aggressively, nor in an impolite manner. Angry women are difficult to work with. Also, wealth is an embarrassment; always I pretend it was an accidental acquisition no matter how hard I worked to ensure security.

I CAN SPEAK OUT ON CAUSES I BELIEVE IN . . . by changing my online avatar and attending up to two peacefully organized gatherings (*protest* is such a combative word).

I SHOULD HAVE CHILDREN, AND THEY WILL BE MY LIFE. The rules change monthly on child-rearing, so I'll be sure to scan all the latest studies of juvenile and formative psychology every six weeks. For now, as is the fashion, I'll use no child care, nor homeschooling, nor private school, nor prepackaged foods, nor helicoptering; and when I "punish," I will be grateful, because my child's purposely flushing my grandmother's diamond ring down the toilet has allowed us a "teachable moment." #BLESSED!

Now. Breathe in and feel that deeply. If it's a life that you can manage, great! Go forth and slay in a most amenable and attractive manner.

But if you find these requirements unspeakable, untenable, and an absolute insult not only to your humanity but also to the very core of reality, take action. Like the ill-fitting women before you who refused to bend. Pick up the tool of destruction that best fits the shape of your hand and your life. Cut strings, chink away at walls, take a pickaxe to the bricks or a blowtorch to the steel. Dig through the very earth you stand on, if you need to.

Be fantastic. Be dreadful. Make awful and brilliant mistakes. Be selfish and generous. Brave and cowardly. That's what humans who make differences do; create drops of change until they swell into a wave strong enough to cause planetary motion.

When the world tells you that you don't fit, agree most cheerfully with the world.

They're right.

You *are* one of the lucky ones.

ACKNOWLEDGMENTS

Thank you to Jessica Papin, who can sell problematically themed nonfiction, during a pandemic shutdown, from three oceans away. Who solves any problem with a turn of phrase so delicate it's a actually a pirouette of phrase. The mondo-bizzaro version of everything I am who nevertheless has never faltered in her faith that my strange work is good work.

And to Gus. Mary had Andrewuk, Lena had Albert, Lillian had Frank. I have you. For half my life, you have been the solid and nutrient earth that sustains me and everything I love, so we may grow. I love you, sweet man.

FURTHER READING

Many of the women profiled in this book have tremendous fans who love them and wrote all they could about them, despite a scarcity of information. I relied generously on their work.

Hetty: The Genius and Madness of America's First Female Tycoon, by Charles Slack, reprint (New York: Ecco, 2004)

Poker Alice Tubbs: The Straight Story, by Liz Morton Duckworth (Palmer Lake, CO: Filter Press, 2018)

A Perfect Fit: How Lena "Lane" Bryant Changed the Shape of Fashion, by Mara Rockliff and Juana Martinez-Neal (New York: Clarion Books, 2022)

Winifred Black/Annie Laurie and the Making of Modern Nonfiction, by Katherine H. Adams and Michael L. Keene (Jefferson, NC: McFarland, 2015)

Making Time: Lillian Moller Gilbreth—A Life Beyond "Cheaper by the Dozen," by Jane Lancaster (Boston: Northeastern University Press, 2004)

Ida: A Sword among Lions: Ida B. Wells and the Campaign against Lynching, by Paula Giddings (New York: HarperCollins, 2009)

Dr. Martha Hughes Cannon: Suffragist, Senator, Plural Wife, by Constance L. Lieber (Salt Lake City: Signature Books, 2022)

Notorious Victoria: The Uncensored Life of Victoria Woodhull—Visionary, Suffragist, and First Woman to Run for President, by Mary Gabriel (Chapel Hill, NC: Algonquin Books, 1998)

WORKS CONSULTED

Abbott, Leonard D. "The Incarnation of Labor's Struggle." *Everyman*, April 1925, n.p.

Adamic, Louis. "Morons of Los Angeles." *Haldeman-Julius Monthly* 4, no. 6 (November 1926): n.p.

Adams, Katherine H., and Michael L Keene. *Winifred Black/ Annie Laurie and the Making of Modern Nonfiction*. Jefferson, NC: McFarland, 2015.

"Aida Walker as Salome." *New York Tribune*, July 29, 1912. https://digitalcollections.nypl.org/items/75d82a22-8e5c-a51e-e040-e00a180663b6.

"Aimee Semple McPherson, Famous Los Angeles Evangelist, Dies at 53." *Belleville News-Democrat*, September 27, 1944, n.p.

"American Doctress in London." *Buffalo Commercial*, December 21, 1866, n.p.

"Angus M. Cannon Arrested." *Idaho Statesman*, July 9, 1899, n.p.

Backus, Paige Gibbons. "Dr. Mary Edwards Walker: Surgeon, Feminist, Suffragist." American Battlefield Trust website, January 25, 2021.https://www.battlefields.org /learn/articles/dr-mary-edwards-walker-surgeon-feminist -suffragist.

The Beecher-Tilton War: Theodore Tilton's Full Statement of the Great Preacher's Guilt; What Frank Moulton Had to Say: The Documents and Letters from Both Sides. Ann Arbor, MI: University of Michigan Library, 2005.

Bill, Laurel. "The Queen of Reindeer: The Remarkable Story of Mary Makrikov." *Alaska*, March 9, 2018. https://alaska magazine.com/authentic-alaska/culture/the-queen -of-reindeer/.

"Biography of Angus Munn." Washington County Historical Society website. https://wchsutah.org.

Black, Winifred. "The Tragedy of Maternity." *Parsons Daily Sun*, February 5, 1907, n.p.

Bodie, Matthew T. "Mother Jones Meets Gordon Gekko: The Complicated Relationship Between Labor and Private Equity." *University of Colorado Law Review* 79 (2008): 1317.

Brandman, Mariana. "Elizabeth Packard." National Women's History Museum, 2021. https://www.womenshistory .org/education-resources/biographies/elizabeth-packard.

Branson, Roy. "Ellen G. White, Racist or Champion of Equality." *Review and Herald* 147 (1970): 2–3.

"Brisbane Plot Leased." *New York Times,* September 20, 1916. https://www.nytimes.com/1916/09/20/archives/the -real-estate-field-brisbane-plot-leased-with-new-building -for.html.

"British Consider Barring Mrs. McPherson." *New York Times,* September 29, 1928, 1.

Brooks, Maria. "The Reindeer Queen: The True Story of Sinrock Mary." Alexander Street video, 2000. https:// video.alexanderstreet.com/watch/the-reindeer-queen -the-true-story-of-sinrock-mary.

Bullough, Vern L. "Merchandising the Sanitary Napkin: Lillian Gilbreth's 1927 Survey." *Signs: Journal of Women in Culture and Society* 10, no. 3 (spring 1985): 615–27.

Burton, Wilbur Arthur. "Ellen White." In *A History of the Mission of Seventh-Day Adventist Education, 1844-1900,* n.p. Lawrence: Kansas State University Press, 1987.

Cannon, Martha Hughes. *Letters from Exile: The Correspondence of Martha Hughes, 1886–1888,* ed. Constance L. Lieber and John Sillito. Salt Lake City: Signature Books, 1989.

Carey, Ernestine Gilbreth. *Belles on Their Toes*. New York: Crowell, 1950.

"Carrie Nation." *The Portal to Texas History*, University of North Texas Libraries website, April 2022. https://texas history.unt.edu/ark:/67531/metapth1100/.

"Carrie Nation Aids Drunkards' Wives." *New York Times*, August 11, 1904. https://www.nytimes.com/1904/08/11 /archives/carrie-nation-aids-drunkards-wives.html.

"Carrie Nation Like Bulldog." *Los Angeles Evening Express*, June 4, 1931, n.p.

"Carry a Nation." Kansas Historical Society website, June 2010. https://www.kshs.org/kansapedia/carry-a-nation /15502.

"Celesta Geyer a.k.a. Dolly Dimples—Former Circus Fat Lady." Old Picture New View, YouTube video, 2021. https://www.youtube.com/watch?v=_5BaXLVohws.

"Cherry Sisters in Their Final Appearance Recall Their Early Triumphs." *Cedar Rapids Gazette*, June 19, 1918, n.p.

Churchill, Frank C. *Reports on the Condition of Educational and School Service and the Management of Reindeer Service in the District of Alaska*. Washington, DC: U.S. Government Printing Office, 1906.

Clark, Sam. "The Truth about Hetty Green." *Belleville News-Democrat*, August 16, 1916, n.p.

"About the Society." Congressional Medal of Honor Society website, n.d. https://www.cmohs.org/.

Cooper, Courtney Ryley. "Easy Come, Easy Go." *Saturday Evening Post*, December 3, 1927, n.p.

"Dolly Dimples, 555-Pound Fat Lady, Now Trim 125." *Spokesman Review* (Spokane, WA), August 7, 1955, 19.

Duckworth, Liz Morton. *Poker Alice Stubbs: The Straight Story*. Palmer Lake, CO: Filter Press, 2018.

Dufresne, Nancy. "Aimee's Castle: My New Home." *Dufresne Ministries Monthly Newsletter*, September 2015.

Edwards, L. F. "Dr. Mary Edwards Walker (1832–1919): Charlatan or Martyr?." *Ohio State Medical Journal* 54, no. 10 (1958): 1296.

El-Hai, Jack. "The Shaming of the Cherry Sisters." *Longreads*, October 6, 2016. https://longreads.com/2016/10/06/the-shaming-of-the-cherry-sisters/.

"Ellen White and Black People." Black Seventh-day Adventist History website, n.d. https://www.blacksdahistory.org/ellen-white-and-blacks.

"Ellen White: Early Years." Lineage Journey website. https://lineagejourney.com/read/ellen-white-early-years.

"End of the Packard Matter." *Chicago Evening Post*, June 7, 1869, n.p.

Eschner, Kat. "The Peculiar Story of the Witch of Wall Street." *Smithsonian*, November 21, 2017.

"Evening World." *Evening Post*, (Wellington, NZ) August 15, 1912. https://paperspast.natlib.govt.nz/newspapers/evening-post/1912/08/15.

"Female Doctor in Manchester." *Brooklyn Daily Eagle*, October 26, 1866, n.p.

Field, Mary. "She Stirreth Up the People." *Everyman*, April 1925, n.p.

"First Senator Among Women: Annie Laurie Interviews Martha Hughes Cannon of Utah." *San Francisco Examiner*, November 9, 1896, n.p.

Ford, Carol. "Hetty Green: A Character Study." *National* magazine, September 1905, n.p.

"Four Freaks from Iowa." *New York Times*, November 17, 1896. https://www.nytimes.com/1896/11/17/archives/four-freaks-from-iowa-they-presented-a-spectacle-more-pitiable-than.html.

Foursquare Church. "Who Is Aimee Semple McPherson?" YouTube video, 2010. https://www.youtube.com/watch?v=ilH0xX3ZYD4.

"Fun in New York." *Daily Memphis Avalanche*, May 16, 1872, n.p.

Gabriel, Mary. *Notorious Victoria: The Uncensored Life of Victoria Woodhull—Visionary, Suffragist, and First Woman to Run for President.* Chapel Hill, NC: Algonquin Books, 1998.

Gänzl, Kurt-Fredrich. "'In Dahomey': One of the First American Black Musical Hits." In *Encyclopedia of the Musical Theatre*, 2nd ed., n.p. New York: Schirmer, 2001.

Gavin, Jennifer, "Take Those Comics Seriously." Library of Congress website, March 20, 2012. https://blogs.loc.gov/loc/2012/03/take-those-comics-seriously/.

Ge, Long, et al. "Comparison of Dietary Macronutrient Patterns of 14 Popular Named Dietary Programmes for Weight and Cardiovascular Risk Factor Reduction in Adults: Systematic Review and Network Meta-Analysis of Randomised Trials." *British Medical Journal* 369 (2020): n.p.

Giddings, Paula J. *Ida: A Sword Among Lions: Ida B. Wells and the Campaign against Lynching.* New York: HarperCollins, 2009.

Gilbreth, Frank Bunker, and Ernestine Gilbreth Carey. *Cheaper by the Dozen.* New York: Thomas Y. Crowell, 1948.

Gilbreth, Frank Bunker, and Lillian Moller Gilbreth. *Fatigue Study: The Elimination of Humanity's Greatest Unnecessary Waste, a First Step in Motion Study*. New York: Macmillan, 1919.

Gilbreth, Lillian Moller. *The Psychology of Management: The Function of the Mind in Determining, Teaching and Installing Methods of Least Waste*. New York: Sturgis & Walton, 1914.

Gilbreth Network website: https://gilbrethnetwork.tripod.com/front.html.

Glass, Andrew. "Carrie Nation Smashes a Kansas Bar." *Politico*, December 27, 2017.

Goldsmith, Bonnie Zucker. *Dr. Mary Edwards Walker: Civil War Surgeon & Medal of Honor Recipient*. Minneapolis: Abdo Publishing, 2010.

Griffin, Lynne, and Kelly McCann. *The Book of Women: 300 Notable Women History Passed By*. New York: Adams Media, 1992.

Grimley, Naomi. "The Mysterious Disappearance of a Celebrity Preacher." BBC News, November 25, 2014. https://www.bbc.com/news/magazine-30148022.

Gurowitz, Margaret. "The Product That Dared Not Speak Its Name." Kilmer House website, February 7, 2008.

https://www.kilmerhouse.com/2008/02/the-product
-that-dared-not-speak-its-name.

Hall-Patton, Mark. "When Game of Faro Was King." You-
Tube video, May 20, 2016. https://www.youtube.com
/watch?v=TbRowtmeVLU.

Halper, Donna. "Marie Zimmerman: The First Woman
Radio Station Owner." *Broadcasters' Desktop Resource*, July
29, 2010.

"Hammerstein's Roof Garden." *New York Tribune*, August 4,
1912, n.p.

Hartog, Hendrik. "Mrs. Packard on Dependency." Wiscon-
sin Legal History Program, Institute for Legal Studies,
1988.

"Hetty's Daughter Dies." *Life* magazine, February 19, 1951,
p. 136.

Hill, Constance Valis. *Tap Dancing America: A Cultural History*.
New York: Oxford University Press, 2010.

Hilliker, Jim. "The History of KFSG." *Los Angeles Radio People*,
2003. https://jeff560.tripod.com/kfsg.html.

"History of Foursquare." Foursquare Church website, n.d.
https://www.foursquare.org.

"History of Magazines." Magazine Newsstand website, n.d. https://magazinenewsstand.com/history-of-magazines -digital.

Hubbard, Jessica. "A 'Woman's Mission': Victorian Ideals of Womanhood in the Anti-Lynching Movement, 1892–1922." Master's thesis, City University of New York, 2014.

"Ida B. Wells and the Campaign against Lynching." Bill of Rights Institute website. https://billofrightsinstitute.org /essays/ida-b-wells-and-the-campaign-against-lynching.

Iornsby, John Aililan. "Queen of the Innuit." *Sunday* magazine, December 3, 1905, n.p.

Irwin, Virginia. "Success Story of a Seamstress." *Saint Louis Post*, February 8, 1948, n.p.

Jackson, Veronica. "Restructuring Respectability, Gender, and Power: Aida Overton Walker Performs a Black Feminist Resistance." *Journal of Transnational American Studies* 10, no. 1 (2019): n.p.

Jacobs, Becky. "Martha Hughes Cannon's Life Goes Deeper than Her Role as First Female State Senator." *Salt Lake Tribune*, October 11, 2020, n.p.

Kallan, Richard A. "Style and the New Journalism: A Rhetorical Analysis of Tom Wolfe." *Communications Monographs* 46, no. 1 (1979): 52–62.

Keist, Carmen and Sara B. Marcketti. "'The New Costumes of Odd Sizes': Plus-Sized Women's Fashions, 1910–1924." *Clothing and Textiles Research Journal* 31, no. 4 (October 2013): 259–74. https://journals.sagepub.com/doi/10.1177/0887302X13503184.

"Kidnapped Evangelist in Perjury Inquiry." *New York Times*, July 30, 1926.

King, Gilbert. "The Incredible Disappearing Evangelist." *Smithsonian*, June 17, 2013, n.p.

Klaber, Louise. "Lane Bryant Malsin." In *Shalvi/Hyman Encyclopedia of Jewish Women*, n.p. https://jwa.org/encyclopedia/article/malsin-lane-bryant.

Klifto, Kevin M., Amy Quan, and A. Lee Dellon. "Mary Edwards Walker (1832–1919): Approach to Limb Salvage Therapy." *Wound Repair and Regeneration* 27, no. 3 (2019): 285–287.

Lancaster, Jane. *Making Time: Lillian Moller Gilbreth—A Life beyond "Cheaper by the Dozen."* Boston: Northeastern University Press, 2004.

"Lane Bryant Mid-Winter Catalogue." Lane Bryant website, 1941. https://www.lanebryant.com/.

"Lane Bryant Show Marks 50th Year." *New York Times*, September 1, 1954. https://www.nytimes.com/1954/09/01/archives/lane-bryant-show-marks-50th-year.html.

Lange, Alexandra. "The Woman Who Invented the Kitchen." *Slate*, October 25, 2012.

Lange, Katie. "Meet Dr. Mary Walker: The Only Female Medal of Honor Recipient." *Department of Defense News*, March 7, 2017, n.p.

Laurie, Annie. "A City's Disgrace." *San Francisco Examiner*, January 19, 1890. https://undercover.hosting.nyu.edu/s /undercover-reporting/item/13090.

Laurie, Annie. "Lovers' Troubles Are Answered by Annie Laurie." *San Bernardino County Sun*, December 14, 1924, n.p.

Lewis, Arthur H. *The Day They Shook the Plum Tree*. New York: Harcourt, Brace & World, 1963.

Lieber, Constant L. *Dr. Martha Hughes Cannon: Suffragist, Senator, Plural Wife*. Salt Lake City: Signature Books, 2022.

Lipka, Michael. "The Most and Least Racially Diverse US Religious Groups." Pew Research Center, July 17, 2015.

Los Angeles Times Photographic Collection. Updated August 1926. https://digital.library.ucla.edu/catalog?f%5Bmem-ber_of_collections_ssim%5D%5B%5D=Los+Angeles +Times+Photographic+Collection&per_page=100&sort =title_alpha_numeric_ssort+asc.

"Lost 410 Pounds." *Corpus Christi Caller-Times*, August 7, 1955, n.p.

Majors, Monroe Alphus, et al. *Noted Negro Women: Their Triumphs and Activities*. Chicago: Donohue & Henneberry, 1893.

Manesse, Alana Miller. *Women of the USU*. Logan, UT: Utah State University Press, 2020.

McMillen, Margot Ford, and Carlynn Trout. "Carrie A. Nation." State Historical Society of Missouri. https://historicmissourians.shsmo.org/carry-nation/website.

"McPherson-Bogard Debate between Aimee McPherson and Dr. Ben M. Bogard on Miraculous Divine Healing." Church of Christ in Zion, Illinois, website, May 22, 1934. https://www.padfield.com/acrobat/debates/bogard.pdf.

"Miracles of Aimee Semple McPherson: When Sister Aimee Came to Town." *Pentecostal Theology*, April 15, 2019, n.p.

"Miscellaneous." *Buffalo Commercial*, February 16, 1866, p. 1.

"Mister Hetty Green." *Saint Paul Globe*, September 11, 1898, n.p.

Mobley, Tianna. "Ida B. Wells-Barnett: Anti-Lynching and the White House." White House Historical Association, April 9, 2021. https://www.whitehousehistory.org/ida-b-wells-barnett-anti-lynching-and-the-white-house.

Morgan, Douglas. "1919 and the Rise of Black Adventism." *Spectrum*, June 28, 2019, n.p.

"Mother Jones, Fiery Crusader, Defied Machine Guns to Win." *Rock Island Argus*, December 6, 1930, n.p.

"Mother Jones Is Deported at Own Request." *Daily Argus-Leader* (Sioux Falls, SD), March 16, 1914, n.p.

Mother Jones." Museum website. https://www.motherjones museum.org.

Mott, Frank Luther. *A History of American Magazines: 1741–1850*, vol. 1. Cambridge, MA: Harvard University Press, 1938.

"Mottled Record of 'Mother Jones,' Labor Agitator" *Deseret News*, (Salt Lake City, UT)April 30, 1904, n.p.

Murray, R. C. "Williams and Walker, Comedians." *Colored American Magazine*, vol. IX, no. 3 (September 1905): n.p.

Nation, Carry Amelia. *The Use and Need of the Life of Carry A. Nation*. Topeka, KS: F. M. Steves & Sons, 1904.

"Native Victorian Returns Here to Show Own Show." *Victoria Advocate*, February 12, 1941, n.p.

"On Santa Claus' Stock Farm." *San Francisco Call*, January 5, 1908, n.p.

Packard, Elizabeth P. W. "Modern Persecution, or, Insane Asylums Unveiled." New York: Pelletreau & Raynor, 1873. Reprint by Hardpress, 2021.

Packard, Elizabeth P. W. *Marital Power Exemplified in Mrs. Packard's Trial, and Self-Defence from the Charge of Insanity: Or, Three Years' Imprisonment for Religious Belief, by the Arbitrary Will of a Husband, with an Appeal to the Government to So Change the Laws as to Afford Legal Protection to Married Women. Packard v. Packard Case.* Alpha Editions, 2022: First published in 1867.

Papachristou, Judith. *Women Together: A History in Documents of the Women's Movement in the United States.* New York: Knopf, 1976.

Parton, Mary Field. *Autobiography of Mother Jones.* Chicago: Charles H. Kerr, 1925.

"Pastor Is Sentenced." *New York Times*, December 21, 1928.

Paterson, Kerry K. "A Fresh Look at Rape During the U.S. Civil War." Women's Media Center website, May 9, 2013.

"Performer Celesta Geyer Dies." *Cincinnati Post*, February 23, 1982, n.p.

"Personal." *Boston Evening Transcript*, April 13, 1896, n.p.

"Personal." *Buffalo Courier*, December 14, 1866, p. 4.

"Playing One Night Stands." *Topeka State Journal*, February 1, 1889, n.p.

"Poker Alice Calm as Pardon Comes." *Rapid City Journal*, December 2, 1930, n.p.

"Poker Alice Seeks Pardon." *Daily Argus-Leader* (Sioux Falls, SD) November 14, 1928, n.p.

"Poker Alice Tubbs." *Evansville Press*, March 10, 1929, n.p.

"Poker Alice Tubbs Dies at Age of 77." *New York Times*, February 28, 1930. https://www.nytimes.com/1930/02/28/archives/poker-alice-tubbs-dies-at-age-of-77-was-equally-adept-at-cards-and.html.

"Poker Alice's Career Had Pathetic, Stormy Events." *Rapid City Journal*, June 21, 1953, n.p.

"Popularity of Cherry Sisters Does Not Dim with Years." *Cedar Rapids Evening Gazette*, May 26, 1916, n.p.

"Press: Annie Laurie." *Time* magazine, October 28, 1935, n.p. https://content.time.com/time/subscriber/article/0,33009,847544,00.html.

"Queen of the Cake Walk." YouTube video. https://www.youtube.com/watch?v=qvAJFQhpuaI.

Rea, Walter T. *The White Lie*. Turlock, CA: M & R Publications, 1982.

"A Reindeer Queen." *Brooklyn Daily Eagle*, January 11, 1902, n.p.

"Reindeer Queen of Alaska Rules over Wide Domain." *Salt Lake Tribune*, February 14, 1902, n.p.

"Riot at Pittsburg Labor Meeting." *Scranton Republican*, January 18, 1902, n.p.

Roen, Samuel. *Diet or Die: The Dolly Dimples Weight Reducing Plan.* New York: Frederick Fell, 1968.

Roen, Samuel. "For Dolly Dimples, Fat City Was No Picnic." *Detroit Free Press*, October 4, 1981, n.p.

Rudwick, Elliott M., and August Meier. "Black Man in the 'White City': Negroes and the Columbian Exposition, 1893." *Phylon* 26, no. 4 (1965): 354–361.

Rydell, Robert W., ed. *The Reason Why the Colored American Is Not in the World's Columbian Exposition: The Afro-American's Contribution to Columbian Literature.* Urbana: University of Illinois Press, 1999.

San Francisco Board of Supervisors. San Francisco Municipal Reports (1892).

"Saved Pennies, Now World's Richest Woman." *Decatur Herald*, December 29, 1905, n.p.

"Says She 'Doubled' for Mrs. M'pherson." *New York Times*, September 14, 1926.

"Scientific Specialization in Stouts: A Malsin Believes That It Is Impossible to Fit All Types of Stouts According to a Single Standard." *Women's Wear Daily*, July 9, 1915, n.p.

Scionti, Julianna. "Political Influence Before Women's Suffrage: Insight into a Wider Definition of Political Engagement." Thesis, Department of American Studies, Brandeis University, 2019.

"Seven-Day Adventists: The Bible Not Sufficient. Ellen G. White, Their Prophetess and Seer." *Worthington Advance*, April 30, 1891, n.p.

Shaplen, Robert. "The Beecher-Tilton Affair." *The New Yorker*, June 12, 1954, n.p.

Shmerling, Robert H. "When Dieting Doesn't Work." *Harvard Health*, May 26, 2020, n.p.

Simon, James Johnson Koffroth. "Twentieth-Century Inupiaq Eskimo Reindeer Herding on Northern Seward Peninsula, Alaska." Ph.D. dissertation, University of Alaska Fairbanks, 1998.

Simonson, George Montfort. "Pastels in Sage-Green and Gold." *Godey's* magazine, November, 1895, n.p.

Slack, Charles. *Hetty: The Genius and Madness of America's First Female Tycoon*. Reprint. New York: Ecco, 2004.

Smith, Uriah. *Our Country's Future: The United States in the Light of Prophecy*. Battle Creek, MI: Seventh-day Adventist Publishing Association, 1884.

Stilwell, Blake. "Why the United States Revoked Hundreds of Medals of Honor." Military.com, n.d. https://www.military.com/history/why-united-states-revoked-hundreds-of-medals-of-honor.html..

Stoddart, Anne, ed. *Topflight: Famous American Women*. Tualatin, OR: Norwood Press, 1946.

"Strong-Minded Women." *New York Daily Herald*, July 21, 1867, n.p.

"Summary of Domestic News." *The Manchester Guardian*, May 9, 1893, 7.

Syme, Eric Douglas. "Seventh-Day Adventist Concepts on Church and State." Ph.D. dissertation, American University, 1969.

Taylor, Angela. "A Store That's a Haven If You're Pregnant, Tall or Plumpish." *New York Times*, April 20, 1970. https://www.nytimes.com/1970/04/20/archives/a-store-thats-a-haven-if-youre-pregnant-tall-or-plumpish.html.

Terrell, Ellen. "Hetty Green the 'Witch of Wall Street' Was Born." Library of Congress Research Guides, This Month in Business History, November 2016. https://

guides.loc.gov/this-month-in-business-history/november/hetty-green-born.

Teske, Anastasia. "Carrie Amelia Moore Nation." *Encyclopedia of Arkansas* blog, December 5, 2022. https://encyclopediaofarkansas.net/entries/carrie-amelia-moore-nation-2514/.

Tilton, Theodore. *Biography of Victoria C. Woodhull*. New York: The Golden Age Publishers, 1871.

"Time Machine: The Cherry Sisters." *Cedar Rapids Gazette*, January 3, 2015. https://www.thegazette.com/news/time-machine-the-cherry-sisters/.

"To Cakewalk Successfully One Must Be Light-Hearted." *Indianapolis News*, March 28, 1903, n.p.

Todd, Kim. "These Women Reporters Went Undercover to Get the Most Important Scoops of Their Day." *Smithsonian*, November 2016, n.p.

Tucker, David M. "Miss Ida B. Wells and Memphis Lynching." *Phylon* 32, no. 2 (1971): 112–122.

"$2,500 Check to Judge a 'Love Offering.'" *New York Times*, January 29, 1929.

"Two Notable Careers: Larned Chronoscope." Kansas Historical Society website, April 23, 1897. https://www.kshs.org/p/the-story-of-fort-larned/13139.

"U.S. Diplomacy and Yellow Journalism 1895–1898. Department of State Office of the Historian website. https://history.state.gov/milestones/1866-1898/yellow -journalism.

"Utah Polygamy Case." *Muscatine Semi-Weekly News Tribune*, July 25, 1899, n.p.

"Utah Woman Who Is Running against Her Husband for the Office of State Senator." *Sun Journal* (Lewiston, ME) October 28, 1896, n.p.

"Victoria's Deeds in Gay Paris." *Philadelphia Inquirer*, November 30, 1891, p. 7.

"Victoria Woodhull and the Free Love Movement: The History You Didn't Learn." YouTube video, 2022. https:// www.youtube.com/watch?v=y3QpvQG3hP4.

Walker, Aida Overton. "Colored Men and Women on the Stage." *Colored American Magazine*, n.m., 1905, p. 571.

Walker, Dr. Mary Edwards. "A Female Esculspius." *Buffalo Morning Express*, June 22, 1863, n.p.

"Walking-for-a-Cake." *New York Times*, February 7, 1897. https://www.nytimes.com/1897/02/07/archives /walking-for-a-cake-eleven-couples-competed-and-mr -marshall-and-miss.html.

Walsh, Colleen. "Recalling Another Strange, Historic Election." *Harvard Gazette*, November 2, 2020, n.p.

"Webb's Patio Carnival." *Tampa Bay Times*, January 3, 1943, n.p.

Weeks, Linton. "The Cherry Sisters: Worst Act Ever?" NPR website, June 27, 2015. https://www.npr.org/sections/npr-history-dept/2015/06/27/417439984/the-cherry-sisters-worst-act-ever.

Wells-Barnett, Ida B. *The Collected Works of Ida B. Wells-Barnett*. Oxford: Pergamon Media, 2015.

Wells-Barnett, Ida B. *Southern Horrors: Lynch Law in All Its Phases*. With introductory chapters by Irvine Garland Penn and T. Thomas Fortune. Redditch, UK: Read Books, 2021.

Wheeler, Samuel. "Elizabeth Packard and Mental Health Laws." Illinois Supreme Court Historic Preservation Commission, n.d.

"William Randolph Hearst." History Channel broadcast, November 30, 2021.

"Woman in the Senate." *Detroit Free Press*, November 17, 1896, n.p.

"Woman Suffragists." *Salt Lake Herald*, March 19, 1895, n.p.

"Women's Suffrage in Utah." National Park Service website. https://www.nps.gov/articles/000/women-s-suffrage -in-utah.htm.

Woodhull, Victoria C. "And the Truth Shall Make You Free." Transcript of Speech, Steinway Hall, New York City, November 20, 1871. https://voicesofdemocracy.umd.edu /victoria-c-woodhull-and-the-truth-shall-make-you -free-speech-text/.

Woodhull, Victoria C. "The Rapid Multiplication of the Unfit." Women's Anthropological Society of America, https://www.loc.gov/item/96183519/1891.

Yost, Edna. *American Women of Science*. Philadelphia: Lippincott, 1955.

Yost, Edna. "The First Lady of Engineering: Lillian M Gilbreth." In *Topflight: Famous American Women*, ed. Anne Stoddard, n.p. Tualatin, OR: Norwood Press, 1946.

INDEX

ABOUT THE AUTHOR

THERESE ONEILL is the *New York Times* bestselling author of *Unmentionable: The Victorian Lady's Guide to Sex, Marriage, and Manners* and *Ungovernable: The Victorian Parent's Guide to Raising Flawless Children*. She lives in Oregon with her family.